THE ROAD TO SAN JACINTO

THE ROAD TO SAN JACINTO

Retracing the Route of Sam Houston's Army

DAVE DYER

State House Press
at Schreiner University
Kerrville, TX
325-660-1752
www.mcwhiney.org

Copyright 2022, State House Press
All rights reserved

Cataloging-in-Publication Data

Names: Dyer, Dave, author.
Title: The road to San Jacinto: retracing the route of Sam Houston's army / Dave Dyer.
Description: First edition. | Kerrville, TX: State House Press, 2022. | Includes bibliographical references, illustrations, maps, and index.
Identifiers: ISBN 9781649670120 (soft cover); ISBN 9781649670144 (e-book)
Subjects: LCSH: San Jacinto, Battle of, Tex., 1836. | Texas – History – Revolution, 1835-1836.
Classification: LCC F390 (print) | DCC 976.4

No part of this book may be reproduced in any form unless with written permission from State House Press, except for brief passages by reviewers.

First edition 2022

Cover and page design by Allen Griffith of Eye 4 Design.

Distributed by Texas A&M University Press Consortium
800-826-8911
www.tamupress.com

CONTENTS

	Introduction vii
1	Sam Houston Takes Command 1
2	Houston's First Big Decision 7
3	The Runaway Scrape 13
4	Camp on the Lavaca River 18
5	Private Rhodes has a Bad Day 23
6	Road to Navidad 27
7	Burnham's Ferry 33
8	Traveling in the Rain 41
9	Retreat at the Colorado 45
10	Camping by a Spring 52
11	San Felipe, The Pompeii of Texas 60
12	Muddy Mill Creek 65
13	Victory or Death at Raccoon Bend 71
14	Basic Training on the Brazos River 77
15	Sam Houston Meets the Twin Sisters 81
16	Rendezvous at Donoho's Plantation 86
17	McCarley's Home 90
18	Fork in the Road 93

19	Telge Park, the Capitol of Texas (for a Day)	99
20	Where Did Sam Houston's Army Camp on April 17, 1836?	105
21	Camp Near Harrisburg	111
22	Captain Bachiller Loses His Clothes	116
23	Almost Checkmate	119
24	Camp Safety	122
25	Vince's Bridge	126
26	Capture of Santa Anna	130
	List of Stops	135
	Epilogue	143
	Notes	147
	Bibliography	153
	Index	159

INTRODUCTION

THE TEXAS COUNTRYSIDE is an open-air museum. Places can help you connect with the past just as objects in a museum can. This book is intended to be a guide to encourage individuals to get out and explore.

This book follows Sam Houston's travels from Gonzales to San Jacinto during the Texas Revolution. The story starts on March 11, 1836, when Houston met the approximately three hundred volunteers who formed the core of the army, and the book ends on April 21, 1836, with Houston's overwhelming victory against Santa Anna at San Jacinto. I set out to locate and visit each campsite along the way. Many of them are unmarked, some are forgotten or questionable. This book turns these ignored sites into a resource for appreciating history. In each case, I used primary sources and old maps to come up with the most likely location. Some of Houston's soldiers published accounts of their activities during this trip. These firsthand accounts offer unique insights and also can be a good introduction to researching primary sources in history. This book offers quotations from these primary sources to illuminate the events at each camp site and often provide clues for finding the exact location. These sources also helped put each site into historical context. The overall process involved some fun historical detective work, and I hope you like the outcome.

You will enjoy the trip more than Sam Houston did! He led an underfed army of rebellious amateurs while they were being pursued by Santa Anna's larger professional Mexican Army that was intent on killing him. Capture by the Mexicans meant sure death—all the prisoners taken at the Alamo and Goliad had been executed. Houston's men wanted to stand and fight but Houston insisted on zigzagging evasively across the wet springtime countryside until he was in position for one decisive battle.

You can make the same trip because this book is presented as a self-guided history tour. Each chapter covers one campsite along with maps and GPS coordinates for easy location. In addition, I have recorded each chapter so that they can be conveniently listened to while visiting the site. I suggest reading the chapter prior to the visit and then listening to the recording while there. At each stop, I have tried to understand the circumstances, motivations, strategy, mistakes, sacrifices, and luck that may explain why things are as they are now. You get the thrill of visiting the exact place where Sam Houston was, combined with the excitement of learning about something that few people know. Visiting a peaceful parking lot that was once the site of prior violence ought to be a starting point for understanding and appreciating the world we have inherited.

The chapters are not intended to be a complete account of the history at that site. Rather, they offer insights and motivations for further research by the reader. Doing your own research of the primary sources can provide you with the thrill of discovery. The goal is activity, not passive reading.

Everything I did is repeatable by the reader. I used all publicly available information and did not seek access to any private property. Some of these sites are on private property but they are visible from the road so there is no need to enter. Please do not enter private property as part of this tour.

I started the project for my own enjoyment as a way to get out of the house during the pandemic, but I had so much fun that I decided to write it up for others. I was surprised to find that a guide such as this did not already exist. There are many accounts of the actual battle, but the long arduous journey leading up to it is not as fully covered. Understanding the preparation for the battle adds to our appreciation of Houston's accomplishments and helps view events in their accurate historical context. It is easy to enjoy the success of victory, but we should also know about all the hard work, stress, and strategy that went into making those eighteen minutes of battle a possibility. For history to have a motivational and instructional value, we should also learn about the difficulties leading to the success. This book focuses on that aspect. Sam Houston was an expert at perseverance. The weather was horrible, his men were almost in open mutiny, and his military opponent both outnumbered him and had better equipment and training. He focused on the goal every day and got things done.

I like to research microhistory because I enjoy knowing exactly where things happened and seeing what that space looks like now. Once you understand what happened at an exact spot, it is easier to put that event into a larger historical context. This bottom-up approach to history is a great way to understand the world around us. Local history is accessible, and visiting a site gives you a personal experience with history. My hope with this work is that the reader can make their own connections to some of the events of Texas' past.

HOW TO USE THIS BOOK

There are QR codes in each chapter. Use your smart phone to scan the QR code and access a map to the site and an audio recording of the chapter.

Use the map to find the site and then listen to the chapter while you are there. This should be more convenient than reading a book during your visit. Google Maps allows you to check in to each location to show that you visited.

If this book is being used as part of a Texas history course, students can share each location they visited with their teacher using the Google Location Sharing capability, or one of numerous geocaching or navigation apps. The structure of this book provides an easy, low-cost way to add a field trip to the course without the overhead of organizing a traditional field trip. The feedback from the site helps the instructor evaluate the educational value of this project.

From the standpoint of the student, this structure allows a convenient way to schedule a field trip around other obligations. In addition, these visits should motivate further research into historical issues.

You do not need to make your visits in exact chronological order because each site is a stand-alone piece of history, but you can always return and do that later if you find these visits enjoyable. Of course, your understanding of the Texas Revolution may deepen if you make these visits in order, just don't expect to visit them all in one day.

THE ROAD TO SAN JACINTO

1 SAM HOUSTON TAKES COMMAND

MARCH 11, 1836
GONZALES, TEXAS

NOBODY KNEW the new commander but there was lots of speculation and gossip: What will he be like? What will he want me to do? How can I start out on his good side? Why wasn't one of the current leaders picked to head the army? It's not easy for an outsider to show up and take control of an existing organization, especially when that organization is an army and the war has already started.

And then the new leader shows up dressed like a Cherokee Indian with a big feather in his hat. He is a huge guy with a pistol strapped to his side and silver spurs on his high-heeled boots. Sam Houston had everyone's attention when he arrived at Gonzales on the afternoon of March 11, 1836.

One historian provides this description of Houston's demeanor: "His personality was a strange mixture of the qualities of a superstitious, cunning, occasionally ruthless Indian war chief and a warm, kindly, courtly, humorous, civilized gentleman."[1]

Houston knew how to make a dramatic entrance; after all, a former girlfriend convinced him to try acting and he had been a success as a member of the Nashville Dramatic Club. He excelled at comedy roles; he was especially memorable as a drunken hotel porter, but also performed serious drama.² Perhaps acting was a good skill for a successful attorney like Houston.

Now that Houston had the men's attention, he went on to establish his authority. He gathered his three hundred men together, some as young as thirteen, for his introduction. He began by reading from a legal document that he assigned the Texas Declaration of Independence:

> When a government has ceased to protect the lives, liberty and property of the people, from whom its legitimate powers are derived, and for the advancement of whose happiness it was instituted, and so far from being a guarantee for the enjoyment of those inestimable and inalienable rights, becomes an instrument in the hands of evil rulers for their oppression.³

If that sentiment reminds you of the American Declaration of Independence, it ought to. The leaders who fought for Texas' independence openly modeled their activities on the American Revolution, and just as George Washington was in charge of the Continental Army, Sam Houston was put in command of the Texian Army. In fact, when Houston finished reading the Texas Declaration of Independence to his men, he then read the orders that put him in charge. As an attorney, he wanted to assure the men of his legitimate authority.

The Texas Revolution started in Gonzales five months before Houston took command of the army. When the war started, Houston was a lawyer in Nacogdoches who was well-known for his friendship with U.S. President Andrew Jackson and because he previously served as governor of Tennessee. His prior military experience in the War of 1812 made him a valuable asset to the new country of Texas, though he

did not immediately rush to the battle. The Mexicans had demanded return of a small cannon they had lent to the settlers to help frighten away potentially hostile Indians, and the Texians responded with a flag showing that famous defiant phrase, "Come and take it." Of course, the revolution was about much more than a small cannon, but it made a good symbol.

Sam Houston never actually saw the cannon because it was buried in the mud by the time he arrived at Gonzales. The volunteers started to take it to the Alamo, but the carriage broke down and they buried it in the mud near a creek about twenty miles from Gonzales to keep it out of enemy hands.

Where is that cannon now? Wouldn't it be fun to see it up close? It was lost, but not forgotten, for a hundred years until it was found by two teenagers after a big flood in 1936. They did not know the historical significance of the object and left it by the side of a road after dragging it

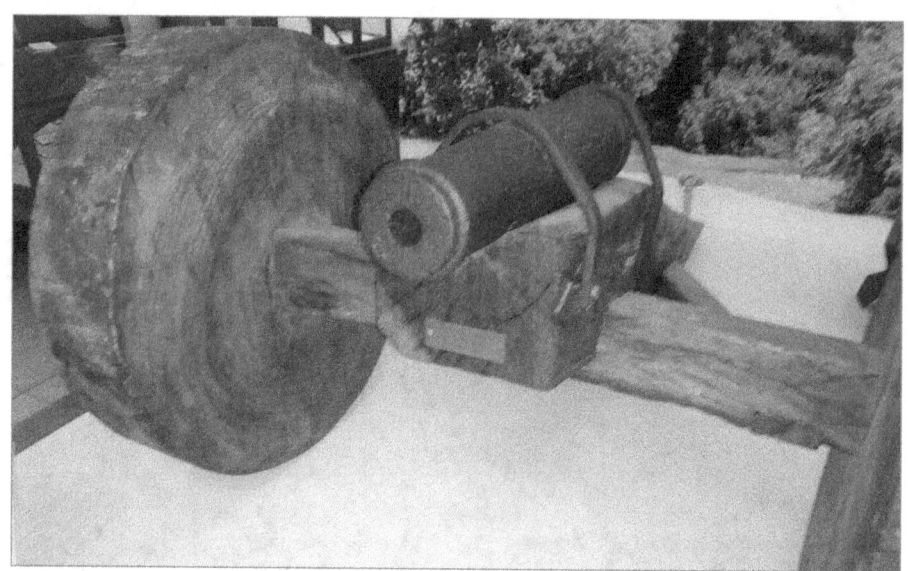

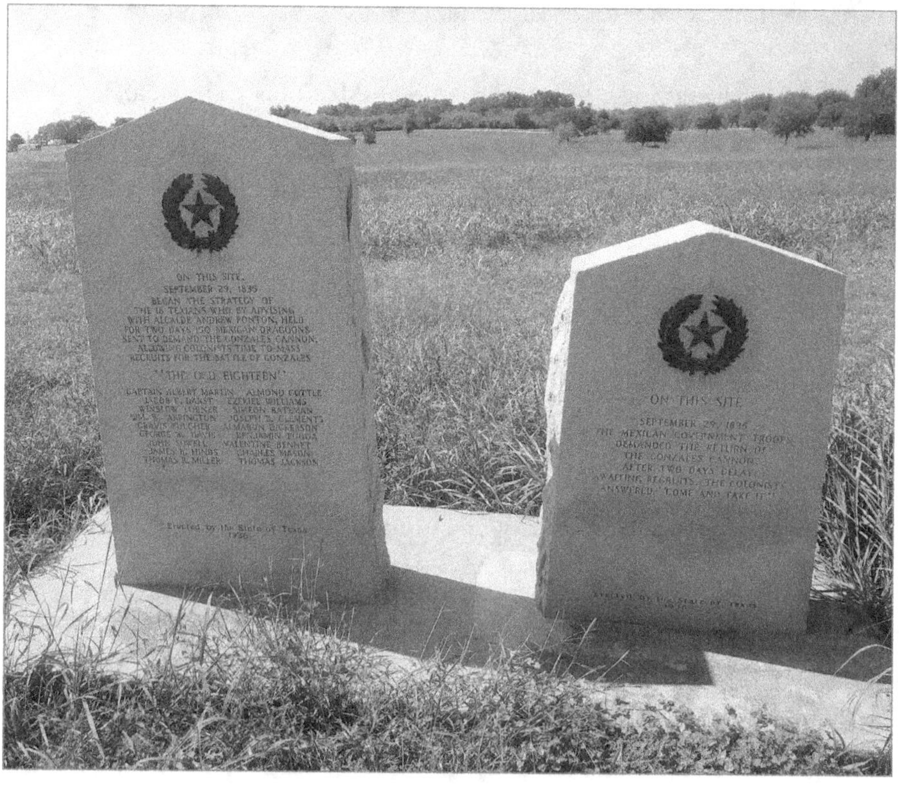
ON THIS SITE,
SEPTEMBER 29, 1835
BEGAN THE STRATEGY OF
THE 18 TEXANS WHO BY ADVISING
WITH ALCALDE ANDREW PONTON, HELD
FOR TWO DAYS 150 MEXICAN DRAGOONS
SENT TO DEMAND THE GONZALES CANNON,
ALLOWING COLONISTS TIME TO MASS
RECRUITS FOR THE BATTLE OF GONZALES
"THE OLD EIGHTEEN"
ON THIS SITE
THE MEXICAN GOVERNMENT TROOPS
DEMANDED THE RETURN OF
THE GONZALES CANNON
AFTER TWO DAYS DELAY
AWAITING RECRUITS, THE COLONISTS
ANSWERED, "COME AND TAKE IT."

out of the mud. It must have been picked up by a rural postman because the cannon spent the next thirty-two years in the basement of a local post office. In 1968, it was bought by a gun collector and passed from hand to hand until it was identified because of the location of a second touchhole that was added after the first one became too large and had to be filled in. Finally, a gun collector donated it to the Gonzales Memorial Museum where it can be seen now. The museum is at 414 Smith Street, Gonzales, Texas. You can get closer to it than Sam Houston ever did!

The site of that first defiant act is located today on County Road 197 just south of the Guadalupe River. As one of the most important historical spots in Texas, two historical markers were created to signify the event, though they both say essentially the same thing. Houston may never have visited this exact spot because his camp was located about a mile to the north.

I went to the location of that camp expecting to find the used car lot that was shown on Google Maps. However, the car lot was gone, and some wooden posts suggest that a fence will soon be built. I walked the empty field where Houston camped 184 years ago hoping to feel some connection. Of course, there is nothing left from his brief stay. Then I saw something in the dirt that was instantly recognizable and highly desirable, a quarter. Then a couple more and some other loose change amounting to an 83-cent haul. Unfortunately, they were all recent dates, not something that fell from Houston's pockets.

COORDINATES FOR HOUSTON'S CAMP
29.497140624988819 / -97.45367276160665

COORDINATES FOR THE GONZALES MEMORIAL MUSEUM
29.504046008046082 / -97.44341149830777

2 HOUSTON'S FIRST BIG DECISION

March 13, 1836
Gonzales, Texas

AFTER SAM HOUSTON took command, he tried to understand what resources he had. His men had little experience and needed both training and better weapons. The army also required better organization and structure. But most importantly, Houston didn't know how many troops were under his command because the status of the siege of the Alamo was unknown. If he could count on those troops, his army would immediately be fifty percent larger. Houston opposed defending the Alamo because he understood the difficulties with defending a stationary position with a small force when surrounded by a much larger force—he was right to be worried. Houston also worried about Col. James Fannin's men in Goliad. With more than four hundred soldiers, Fannin's forces could double the size of Houston's army.

On the morning of March 13, Houston sent Deaf Smith and a couple of other scouts out toward San Antonio to gather news from the Alamo. They only made it about twenty miles before they ran into a small group of survivors, including Susannah Dickenson, her infant daughter, and a black man named Joe who had been Travis' slave. The Alamo was lost, everybody had been killed, and Santa Anna intended to march on Gonzales. They brought the sad news back to Gonzales around 8 p.m.

It is difficult for us to imagine how horrible that news was to the residents of Gonzales. Among the Alamo defenders were thirty-two volunteers from Gonzales. The evening air was filled with the cries of women who became widows and children who found themselves fatherless. In addition, Santa Anna was heading their way.

More than forty years after the events, an eyewitness who was one of Houston's soldiers published this memory: "Many of the citizens of Gonzales perished in this wholesale slaughter of Texans, and I remember most distinctly the shrieks of despair with which the soldiers' wives received news of the death of their husbands. The piercing wails of woe that reached our camps from these bereaved women thrilled me and filled me with feelings I cannot express, nor ever forget."[1]

Later in the day, someone reported seeing four hundred Mexican cavalrymen approaching Gonzales. Houston put his men in position for battle but also sent out a scouting party to find out more about the advancing force. That proved a good move.

Houston's soldier continued his account: "The reconnoitering party, after a short absence, returned and reported the alarm entirely false. A large herd of beef cattle, which were being driven beyond reach of Mexican invasion, had in the distance assumed the appearance of an advancing army."[2]

Houston's small army wanted revenge, and right away. They were ready to stand and fight the larger Mexican force (perhaps two thousand professional soldiers) that had just overrun the Alamo. Some shoeless and armed only with shot guns, they were still eager to fight. Perhaps they were over-confident by the early victories against smaller forces or because of their opinion that the Mexican Army was comprised mainly of derelicts and convicts. It's not hard to imagine how they felt when Houston ordered a retreat, right then, that night. They hated their new commander instantly. What was wrong with him? Was he a coward? Twenty-five of Houston's soldiers immediately deserted.

Houston ordered all the soldiers and civilians to go east immediately. Soldiers were allowed to bring only what they could carry. No tents. No spare food. No barrels of whiskey. The only two cannon owned by the army were thrown in the Guadalupe River. Houston gave three of the army's four wagons to the civilians for their few possessions; the remaining one carried only ammunition. He also gave most of his personal money to the widows. Just before midnight, 374 soldiers started on a 160-mile trip that lasted forty-five days. The group headed down what is now known as St. Louis Street in Gonzales. People can take a walk down this pleasant street and recall those who went before.

Actually, that first big decision by Sam Houston probably saved his army from destruction and kept Texas (which at the time included territory all the way to the Pacific Ocean) from remaining part of Mexico. The United States might be much smaller today if Santa Anna had gotten the quick victory that he intended. Houston's retreat in the face of opposition from his troops proved the right decision.

Why did Houston make the decision to retreat? As a military officer with previous experience, he was probably familiar with the military tactics of French Emperor Napoleon Bonaparte, who managed many successful military campaigns in Europe just twenty years prior. Napoleon emphasized the value of mobility; a smaller force could defeat a larger one by out-maneuvering them to pick the ideal battle conditions. To be maneuverable, the army had to travel light, use light-weight artillery, and eat off the land rather than depend on a long, vulnerable supply chain. The goal should be to have a single decisive battle rather than a string of smaller victories. Houston repeatedly used these tactics throughout the Texas Revolution. His plan was to retreat, train, strengthen and get the Mexicans to extend their supply lines. Most of all, use the advantage of mobility and wait for the enemy to make a mistake, such as dividing their forces.

Ironically, Santa Anna proclaimed himself "The Napoleon of the West" but was defeated by Houston's use of Napoleon's strategy.

People familiar with the Texas Revolution will recognize Napoleon's influence on Houston in the following comments:

> Napoleon placed great emphasis on movement as a part of warfare. This was best demonstrated during his Italian campaign of the 1790s. Taking his troops back and forth across the country, he repeatedly outmaneuvered the Austrians and their Piedmontese

allies. It allowed him to fight battles at a time and place that suited him. . . . He pushed the French military toward field guns which were on average a third lighter than those of their British opponents. This allowed the guns to be moved quickly around the battlefield and used to their best effect. . . . He also focused the power of his guns. Instead of spreading them out to provide support for the infantry, he collected large mobile batteries. Their coordinated firepower could make significant dents in enemy formations. . . . Napoleon aimed to feed his armies from the land rather than transporting large volumes of supplies with them. It had two advantages in supporting his war of movement. Firstly, it meant his armies were unburdened with the weight of supplies and the slowness of wagon trains. Secondly, it made him less dependent on supply lines back to France, making him less vulnerable to enemy maneuvers. . . . Although Napoleon's methods were about outmaneuvering the enemy, his aims were unequivocal. Unlike many of his predecessors, he focused on bringing about the utter destruction of the enemy armies. The goal was not just to defeat or dislodge them. It was to smash them decisively in a single battle, removing their ability to fight and forcing them to negotiation on his terms. . . . The other strategy was the central position. Napoleon used this when he faced more than one enemy or an enemy army that had become divided. By holding a central position, he could split his enemies apart. He would hold one off with a relatively small part of his army, while he defeated the other force.[3]

It's easy to see how Houston incorporated these tactics with his smaller force as well.

Getting There

COORDINATES FOR ST. LOUIS STREET
29.50758478667584 / -97.43121918553393

3 THE RUNAWAY SCRAPE

March 13 and 14, 1836
Gonzales, Texas

SAM HOUSTON translated his decision into immediate action. The evacuation started before midnight because Houston knew they did not have time for the luxury of a good night's sleep or even a meal. Gonzales was sixty miles east of San Antonio, so they had, at most, a sixty-mile head start. With an untrained army restrained by an entire city full of distraught civilians, that head start may have been his only advantage.

Houston had been in charge of the army for two days and he had already ordered them to do something that they clearly didn't want to do, something that gave his men a reason to question his courage. In addition, he had no legal authority to order the civilians to evacuate, but he did it anyway. The civilians gave him less trouble than the army. He let the civilians go first so they could get a head start. When they were out, he ordered his men to burn the town and everything left behind so it would be of no value to the enemy. This may sound cruel, but Houston's strategy was to pull Santa Anna away from his supply base and deny him any new supplies during the trip. The civilians could see their homes burning behind them as they walked into the night towards an unknown destination.

If you think leadership is easy, just put yourself in Houston's shoes.

This mass evacuation was called the Runaway Scrape. Where did the term "Runaway Scrape" come from? There seems to be no documentation to explain the name, but my guess is that some pundit in the army used it as a term of derision for Houston's leadership, and it stuck. Military humor has a long tradition and the disparaging names often stick, such as Fort Blunder for the American fort that was mistakenly built in British territory after the War of 1812.

One of Houston's men wrote his recollections of the event:

> The road was filled with carts and wagons loaded with women and children, while other women, for whom there was no room in the wagons, were seen walking, some of them barefoot, some carrying their smaller children in their arms or on their backs, their other children following barefooted; and other women were again seen with but one shoe, having lost [the] other in the mud; some of the wagons were broken down, and others were bogged in the deep mud. Taken all in all, the sight was the most painful by far, that I ever witnessed. But the cries of the women were still more sidtressing [sic], as they called our attention to their gorlorn [sic] situation, raising their hands to Heaven, and declaring they had lost their all, and knew not where to go; epressing [sic] their preference to die on the road rather than be killed by the Mexicans or Indians.[1]

They traveled all night through open country to the east of Gonzales. Some rode horses but many walked.

They arrived at Peach Creek around dawn after going about ten miles. They had to cross the waterway before taking a two-hour rest. The creek would have been higher than what is shown in the photo on the next page because the area had rain right before the Runaway Scrape. It was easy for the horses. but the soldiers and civilians found themselves wet and covered with mud when they exited the other side.

They were welcomed by a sympathetic local plantation owner, Barthalamew McClure, who supplied breakfast for several hundred people. Their first meal on the road was chunks of freshly slaughtered beef roasted on sticks over an open fire. His plantation on Peach Creek is now called The Houston Oak. Houston's army rested under the tree pictured on page 17 while about ninety more volunteers under Capt. John Bird joined the army bringing the total to just under five hundred. This

large live oak is still alive and can be easily seen from the road, but, since it is on private property, you can't get too close.

While the soldiers and civilians rested, they heard two or three loud explosions coming from the direction of Gonzales. Panic set in as most people assumed it was cannon fire from Santa Anna's army. However, it was probaly just abandoned barrels of whiskey exploding in the fire.[2]

👉 Getting There

COORDINATES FOR PEACH CREEK
29.474035879111124 / −97.31644318981996

COORDINATES FOR SAM HOUSTON OAK
29.476189120616755 / −97.30806981461498

4 CAMP ON THE LAVACA RIVER

MARCH 14, 1836
MOULTON, TEXAS

AFTER A MEAL and a two-hour rest, the men, women, and children of Gonzales, along with the Texas Army, traveled all day on March 14 to reach the next campsite in Moulton, twelve miles from the Houston Oak. At least they got to travel in the daylight this time.

Houston claimed to have eight hundred troops at this point, but the actual number was probably less than five hundred. The exaggeration may have been intentional to help recruiting and improve morale. As the day went on, more refugees joined the ones from Gonzales.

A historical marker built in 1936 in front of an American Legion Hall in Moulton shows where the group stopped for the night. Houston's army encountered some cattle which they slaughtered for the evening meal over a campfire made from the fence posts of a local resident who may have cooperated. Houston's men were exhausted after the march and many just fell to the ground and slept without eating. The reality of war was sinking in.

The source of the Lavaca River is slightly north of Moulton and a narrow stretch of it flows just in back of their camp site. It was almost dry

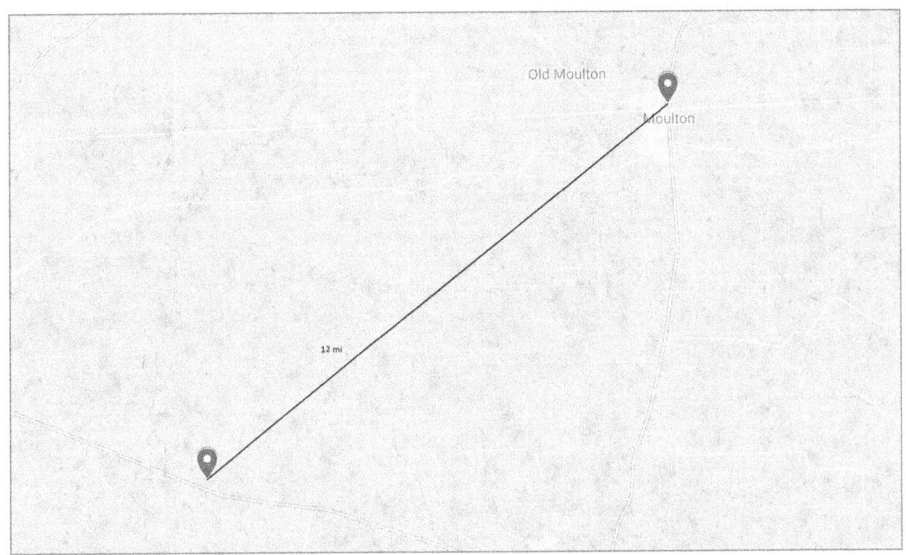

when I visited, but in the wet season like March, there would have been enough water for their horses. They always needed to camp near a source of water because they were traveling light. The army probably camped closer to the water behind where the American Legion building stands today rather than near the marker.

The huge live oak trees behind the building shown in the photo on page 21 may have been around when Houston camped there. Live oaks often live to be five hundred years old if they are in a good location, and this location must be good because there are several of these trees. It is a real treat to see and imagine that these are the same trees that Houston and his men probably saw when they were at the same spot 185 years ago. Live oaks are the strongest and densest of all oak trees. Thankfully, they are no longer harvested for lumber, but they were previously used for shipbuilding. The famous three-masted frigate the USS *Constitution* was nicknamed "Old Ironsides" because cannon balls bounced off her sides during the War of 1812—she was constructed with live oak.[1]

The Road to San Jacinto

The day was hard on everyone, but it was especially difficult for the youngest soldier, thirteen-year-old John Holland Jenkins. He was not able to keep up with the full-grown men as he carried a heavy weapon, ammunition, and his knapsack. The knapsack contained two pounds of bacon wrapped in his blanket.[2] Yum. Houston noticed that the youngster was having difficulty and procured a horse for him to ride. Houston instructed Jenkins to stay near him, but Jenkins was inattentive, as any energetic thirteen-year-old might be, and wandered off ahead of the others. Houston eventually cursed at him just as he would have any grown soldier. Jenkins had his pride hurt and refused to ride anymore. Eventually, Houston sent him home for his own good. Later in life, Jenkins became a Texas Ranger and wrote a memoir of his experiences.

He claimed that he acquired a permanent dislike for Houston and always voted against him.

As is often the case, there is some reasonable doubt that the historical marker for this location is in the correct spot.[3] One of Houston's soldiers who wrote a memoir commented that they camped on the property of Williamson Daniels.[4] As the historical 1896 map on the next page shows, the Daniels property is east of Moulton and farther downriver. It is also on the opposite bank, a better camp site from a military standpoint because it could provide some protection in case the enemy attacked. The location is on the Gonzales and Columbus Road, which adds some credence for this other possible location. It is on private property and not available for a visit.[5]

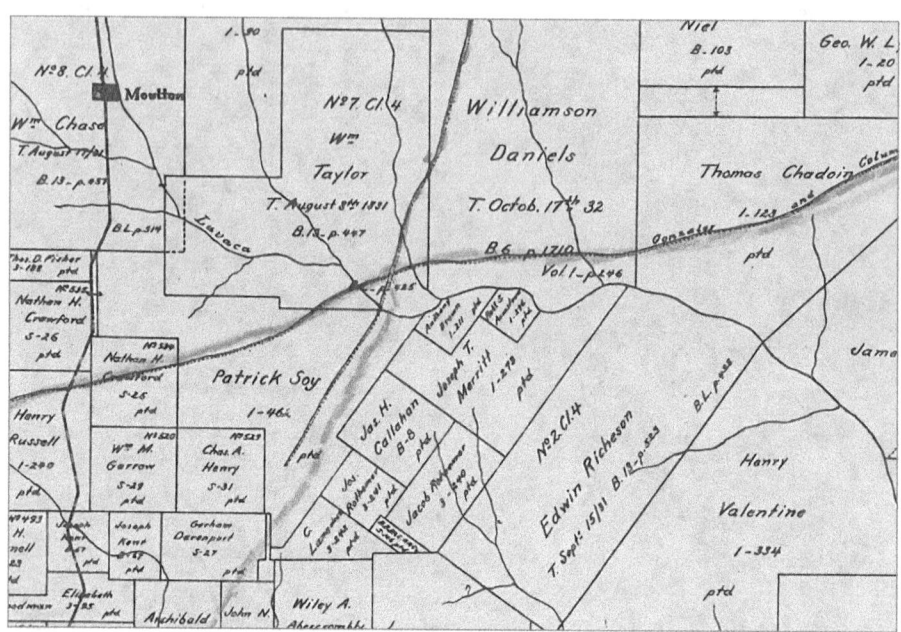

COORDINATES FOR AMERICAN LEGION HALL IN MOULTON
29.579086734780766 / −97.14343121586357

5 PRIVATE RHODES HAS A BAD DAY

MARCH 15, 1836
AT ROCKY CREEK

THERE IS NEVER a good excuse for falling asleep while on guard duty, not even after two days of heavy marching with little sleep. A little carelessness could allow a surprise attack by the enemy, possibly causing the destruction of the army. This being the case, Houston was furious when he found out that one of his soldiers, John Rhodes, had been found sleeping while on guard, and a furious Houston must have been something to see. Houston ordered Rhodes arrested and swore that he would soon be shot. But first, they had to leave the camp on the Lavaca for the next one on the Navidad River. There would be plenty of time to shoot Rhodes that evening, Houston reasoned. After only four days on the job, Houston had ordered the evacuation of the army and the entire town of Gonzales, and was now preparing to have one of his soldiers shot! It certainly had been an eventful four days.

The army spent the night near the Lavaca River on the property of Williamson Daniels shown on the left of the 1853 Lavaca County map (see page 24). The dotted line running horizontally across the map is the old Gonzales-Columbus Road which Houston would have taken. Towards

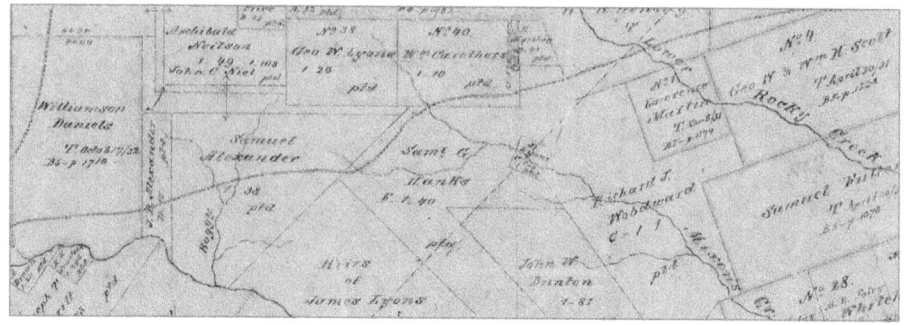

Charles W. Pressler, Lavaca County, map, October 1853, University of North Texas Libraries, The Portal to Texas History, found online at: *https://texashistory.unt.edu/ark:/67531/metapth88766/*.

the right of the map, the Gonzales-Columbus Road crosses Lower Rocky Creek (now called Big Rocky Creek). A state historical marker titled "Route of the Texas Army" is supposed to be at this spot, but it seems to be missing.

One might think that poor John Rhodes would have tried to stay inconspicuous since he was already on Houston's bad side, but he actually managed to get in trouble again that same day, right at this spot.

The army was crossing Lower Rocky Creek when Rhodes paused to take a drink. The column of soldiers behind him bunched up and came to a halt. Houston rode up on his horse and thundered, "Knock him down, God damn him! Standing there holding up the whole army! God damn him! Knock him down." Rhodes got the message and started moving right away. It was enough of an event that Rhodes' commander recalled it word for word when he wrote about it in his memoirs twenty years later.[1]

Despite Houston's anger, he did not shoot Rhodes right then and there. In fact, by the end of the day, Houston pardoned Rhodes and let him live. Houston felt confident that his message had been delivered to the troops. Besides, he needed every man he could get for the coming battle. But don't feel sorry for Rhodes. He stayed with the army all the

way through the Battle of San Jacinto and is now revered as one of the heroes who helped win independence for Texas. He is listed as a member of Captain Kuykendall's regiment on April 21, 1836, as one of the Texans stationed at the camp to guard the baggage.[2]

Houston did have his softer side. That same day he heard about the plight of a blind widow with six children who had missed the Runaway Scrape and been missed by his army. He sent two soldiers back fifteen miles to find her.[3]

When I visited what is now called Big Rocky Creek, the site was a construction project. Luckily, it was late on a Sunday afternoon, the work had stopped, and I was able to get by the heavy equipment for a look at the creek. I did not go down the steep embankment for a drink, but it looked very clear and clean. I even saw a few small fish. No doubt it looked good to Pvt. John Rhodes.

COORDINATES FOR ROCKY CREEK
29.5815407938608878 / -96.91829932873303

6 ROAD TO NAVIDAD

March 15, 1836
Oakland, Texas

AFTER CROSSING what is now known as Big Rocky Creek, the army stayed on the Gonzales Road to the next good water supply on the Navidad River. They arrived around 1 p.m. and stopped for the day on the property of William Thompson, to the joy of the tired soldiers.[1]

The photo on page 28 is a current photo of the land that looked so good to Houston's men. This image is as close as one can get to Houston's camp on Thompson's land because it is all private property and not accessible.

An 1866 map of Lavaca County clearly shows the Gonzales Road crossing the Thompson property and this same road also went through the Williamson Daniels property where the Texans camped the prior night, providing supporting evidence that the army probably took the Gonzales Road. Satellite photos of Thompson's property show no indication of the path hundreds of Texans walked, so it appears nature reclaimed this route.

The portion of the Gonzales Road between Big Rocky Creek and the Navidad River, however, seems to have turned into FM 221. This straight

Joseph Martin, Lavaca County, map, January 30, 1866, University of North Texas Libraries, The Portal to Texas History, found online at: *https://texashistory.unt.edu/ark:/67531/metapth88768/m1/1/*.

gravel road matches up exactly with the path shown on the old map. If you drive down this stretch of FM 221, you would be following Houston's footsteps for about four miles.

Capt. Peyton R. Splane's group of mounted soldiers joined Houston just before arriving at the Navidad, probably somewhere on this road. There were twenty to thirty new volunteers, and some with prior military experience. Houston's plan was working, and the army grew as it retreated. But if other Texans could find the army, so could the Mexicans. That thought gave Houston something more to worry about—perhaps it was time to do something unpredictable.

The parcel of land just south of Thompson's land on the 1866 map was once owned by James Bowie. The original acquisition date was April 20, 1831; Bowie, who was killed at the Alamo, had been a land speculator and this land may have been an investment rather than a home.

The small unincorporated community of Oakland, population eighty, now occupies much of the property. Google Maps showed a small night spot with the intriguing name of "Yaught Club," a place I just had to see. Good thing I did not expect a beer because it seems to have been abandoned for a long time.

But at a longer glance, I found something intriguing. It looked like there was an official historical plaque on the run down Yaught Club. On closer inspection, it was somewhat less than official, but still accurate. It reads: "On March 2, 1836, Texas declared her independence from Mexico, wild Comanches roamed the plains, Rangers protected frontier settlements, and this building was not here yet."

COORDINATES FOR FM 221
29.58603601225505 / -96.91573380947634

7 BURNHAM'S FERRY

March 17–18, 1836
Holman, Texas

THE HOMEMADE MARKER pictured on the next page marks the spot in Colorado County where the Burnham's Ferry historical marker resided for forty-five years after it was spirited away from its original location in Fayette County. The unofficial marker was probably installed in 2010 when the official marker was moved back to its original location. No, the marker location change was not a fraternity prank; some local historians argued about the exact location of Burnham's Ferry and decided to take matters into their own hands.

The historical marker for Burnham's Ferry was installed by the State of Texas on Highway 155 just north of Holman in 1936 as part of the centennial celebration. It was a big granite marker weighing several hundred pounds. All was well for twenty-eight years until a couple of local avocational historians decided that it was in the wrong spot. They were convinced that the real location of Burnham's Ferry was five miles to the south in Colorado County.

Like a couple of mischievous kids, they conveniently forgot to inform the Texas Historical Commission, the owner of the marker, of their belief.

They were so convinced of the marker's incorrect placement that they decided no permission was needed to correct the error. There may have been a wink and a nod from some local county officials when the removal was made. It also seems that they went to the unusual step of grinding off the inscription carved in granite, replacing it with a new etching confirming Colorado County as the proper location. Like they say, you can't always believe everything you read, even if it is written in granite!

Apparently, nobody in Fayette County complained because the marker rested quietly in its new location for forty-five years until someone noticed that a non-existent historical marker was listed on a topographical map of Fayette County. This generated a newspaper article, and they found the missing marker five miles to the south, where it had been for forty-five years. This time, they went through proper channels and enlisted to assistance of the Texas Historical Commission (THC) who,

it seems, also had not noticed the problem for forty-five years. Of course, this added a year to the process. After many meetings, the THC decided to resurface the back of the marker and add a new accurate inscription. In an interesting turn, the THC also decided to leave the Colorado County inscription because, even though inaccurate, it had been a part of the marker for forty-five years and was now part of the history of the marker itself! The new inscription is on the front and the inaccurate one is on the back, making the Burnham's Ferry marker the only two-sided historical marker in Texas.

One final act of bravado by the two rogue historians was revealed when the marker was removed from the base they made for it in 1964; they had put their initials and the date in the base.

Which location is right? Well, it depends. Jesse Burnham may have had two ferry operations. He was an early settler and had lots of land along the Colorado River. The northern one started in 1824 and was the one used

by Houston's army, so the Fayette County location is correct. After the war, Burnham moved to the southern location since Houston had burnt his home to prevent the Mexicans from using it, so the Colorado County location would be accurate for Burnham's southern ferry.

I set out to find the site of the original ferry, but I had a big advantage that the earlier historians didn't have—Google Maps. On the east side of the Colorado River, about the same latitude as the marker, is a small road that goes straight to the river. The name of that road is Burnham's Ferry Road, which logic would state goes to the location of Burnham's Ferry. As more evidence to support this location, we know that Houston went three miles south to John Crier's plantation after crossing: "By two or three o'clock, the last man was ferried over to the east bank of the Colorado, and the same evening the army marched down the river as far as Crier's (2 or three miles)."[1] This statement by one of Houston's soldiers helps confirm my suggestion for the location of Burnham's Ferry. The

Horace L. Upshur, Fayette County, map, 1843, Libraries, The Portal to Texas History, found online at: *https://texashistory.unt.edu/ark:/67531/metapth88545/*.

present-day Crier Creek is about three and a half miles south of Burnham Ferry Road.

More evidence for this location can be found in old maps. The 1843 map (page 37) shows that members of the Burnham family owned plots of land on both sides of the Colorado River. It would be reasonable to assume that the ferry was on his property at this location.

My drive down Burnham Ferry Road took me down the same path that Houston's army must have used after crossing the Colorado River on March 18, and the road has not been improved much since then. It was a rough drive, and when I got to the end, there was a locked gate that kept me from reaching the river.

Given all the controversy over the location of Burnham's Ferry, one might expect to learn that something historically important happened there, but actually it was just a temporary stopping point for the army. Houston reached Burnham's Ferry on the evening of March 17 and camped on the west side, allowing the two hundred or so frightened citizens traveling with him to cross on the ferry first. Houston's army crossed on March 18 and turned south to camp at the home of John Crier, one of Austin's original three hundred settlers. This was the second time that Houston had crossed here. He crossed on March 9 while going west on his way to Gonzales.[2]

Historians have sometimes wondered why he didn't take the shorter more direct route to Beason's Crossing. Mosley Baker, one of Houston's soldiers—and a frequent critic—wrote seven years after the war, "and finally at the remonstrance of many of your officers and the universal complaints of your men, you removed down to Beason's crossing. What possible reason could you have for going to Burnham's crossing? No one that I have ever heard speak on the subject has been able to assign any."[3]

Some have suggested that the zigzag to the north was an attempt to evade the Mexican Army that he knew was chasing him but his knowledge of the area from his prior crossing may have also been a factor. Also, Houston knew he would get a warm reception from John Crier, who soon joined the Texas Army.[4]

Houston destroyed the ferry and buildings at Burnham's upon leaving just as he had done at Gonzales. He wanted to keep any assets from falling into enemy hands.

COORDINATES FOR ORIGINAL AND CURRENT LOCATION IN FAYETTE CO.
29.801997574590878 / −96.79713959502960

COORDINATES FOR STOLEN LOCATION IN COLORADO CO.
29.755464554039584 / −96.73713500553065

COORDINATES FOR BURNHAM FERRY RD.
29.78581375887209 / −96.72351732048868

8 TRAVELING IN THE RAIN

MARCH 19, 1836
NEAR COLUMBUS, TEXAS

ON MARCH 19, Houston's army awoke to rain at John Crier's plantation. Since they were traveling light, they had no tents. The tents had been left in a bonfire at Gonzales to allow rapid movement. They were now safely on the east side of the Colorado River and the ferry had just been destroyed, but they kept moving because Houston feared the safety was temporary.

The rain made Houston's men miserable, but it also brought some advantages. The Colorado River was running full and fast; it became a more valuable barrier against the pursuing Mexicans on the other side. It was impossible to ford and Houston controlled the ferry crossing. Also, it slowed the Mexicans more than it did Houston because the Mexicans carried more supplies and had heavy cannon on carts that kept getting stuck in the mud. Napoleon's tactic of traveling light was paying off.

Houston's army had swelled to perhaps five hundred troops and he was still expecting an additional four hundred men when Fannin's men arrived. That would have given him a respectable army. He considered making his stand at Burnham's, but decided that it would be too easy for the Mexicans to bypass Burnham's by crossing at some point either above or below him and attack from the rear.

Houston's goal was to reach Beason's Crossing at Columbus, about ten miles to the south. This was the main crossing on the most commonly used road, and it was currently unguarded. Since Houston had crossed the Colorado River to the north, he was now approaching Beason's Crossing from the north. He was rushing to get there before the enemy, but the rain slowed his progress and he camped in a thicket of post oak trees before reaching Columbus.

There was some excitement while at this camp. Houston had sent out some scouts, or spies as he called them, to determine the location of the Mexican Army. Houston's spies encountered a group of Mexican spies out looking for the Texans. There was brief skirmish in which one Mexican was killed and another was captured alive. The sword and pistols from the dead Mexican soldier were a big hit among Houston's troops when they were brought back as trophies. Wouldn't it be great to see those items today? The live Mexican soldier was actually more valuable because he provided information about the size and location of the Mexican Army. Houston learned that Santa Anna had divided his army to make it more likely to find the Texans. The nearby force was only 725 men, but they had asked for reinforcements.[1] To Houston, this information meant that his goal of a single decisive battle might be more difficult to achieve because even if he defeated one army, he might have to fight a later battle against the other force. Not good news, but it was best to find out before the armies engaged in fighting.

The exact location of this camp is not known and there are no details in the written accounts from his soldiers that provide enough clues. Later maps of the area show no roads, so it is not likely that any roads existed

while Houston was there. If you want to follow in Houston's footprints, the best option is to take FM 1890 (Shaw's Bend Road) south from Highway 71 to Jerrell Coffee Road. I don't know if Houston camped here, but the thicket of oaks would have looked about like the ones pictured above do today.

There are some small ponds nearby, but Houston could also have gotten water from this small creek that crosses Jerrell Coffee Road. Like several other creeks, this one is named Rocky Creek. At least this one has rocks in it. Houston certainly needed to cross it at some point.

COORDINATES FOR JERRELL COFFEE RD. AND ROCKY CREEK
29.742833030721222 / -96.61723717963098

9 RETREAT AT THE COLORADO

March 20–26, 1836
Columbus, Texas

WHY WOULD YOU retreat when you have a strong defensive position, outnumber the enemy, and your soldiers are eager to fight? Sam Houston had to answer that question for the rest of his life. It was even suggested he could have prevented the massacre of James Fannin's men at Goliad if he had captured enough Mexican troops to pull off a prisoner exchange.

Beason's Crossing (also spelled "Beeson's") controlled a strategic location on the Colorado River. It was too deep to ford, so a ferry was a necessity. Benjamin Beason, one of Stephen F. Austin's original three hundred colonists, founded a ferry boat operation there in 1822. It expanded into a collection of businesses: a sawmill, a boarding house, a grist mill, and a cotton gin. It was the Buc-ee's of its day—a one-stop-shop for everyone who came by. There seems to be no historical account of how clean the restrooms were at Beason's Crossing, but I would rather take my chances with Buc-ee's if given a choice.

On March 19, 1836, Houston's army, accompanied by a large group of civilian refugees as part of the Runaway Scrape, settled in on the eastern side for about a week of training, recruiting, and planning. New recruits, including two hundred Kentucky volunteers under Sidney Sherman, arrived to swell the army's ranks to perhaps 1,500 men. Houston split off one unit to guard the upstream crossing and another to guard the downstream crossing, so Texans controlled a large section of the river. Any Mexican soldiers would be shot at while trying to cross, and they made good targets crowded into a boat. Houston had a great defensive position and he said that he intended to make his stand there.

A unit of the Mexican Army commanded by Gen. Joaquín Ramírez y Sesma was following Houston. Santa Anna had divided his forces to make it easier for at least one of the units to locate Houston. He apparently believed that Houston's band of amateurs would be no match for the Mexican professionals. There were about seven hundred Mexican soldiers who camped about a mile and a half to the west. Houston outnumbered

this group of Mexican soldiers at least two to one. The historical marker on the site (located at the corner of Veteran's Drive and Milentz Street) sits under a flagpole flying the American flag.

If the pond, pictured below, from a nearby golf course is natural, rather than dug just as a water hazard, you can be sure that it provided water for the Mexican Army.

Houston's inexperienced men were so eager for battle that he allowed 150 volunteers to cross the river at night for a surprise attack. The Mexicans saw the raiders and frightened them back over the river with some cannon fire.

Houston kept his army at Beason's Crossing for about a week and trained them every day while he accepted new recruits and studied maps. After a few days, he learned the fate of Fannin's four hundred men at Goliad—they were defeated and captured by Gen. José de Urrea's two thousand soldiers. Houston knew that he had no reinforcements. The news did not sit well with Houston's soldiers, and about two hundred of them left the army immediately.

Suddenly, on the morning of March 26, Houston ordered his men to pack up and pull back. They burned the buildings on the way out so that the Mexicans could not use the resources from Beason's Crossing. The Texans retreated seven miles before camping. The only reason Houston

stopped was to find new grass for the horses and mules. In later years, he said that the battle probably would have been indecisive and that he had no way to evacuate the wounded.

Even if Houston had beaten Sesma decisively, he knew there were other Mexican soldiers nearby. There were fifteen hundred in San Antonio, two thousand in Goliad, and a thousand in Bastrop. Also, Santa Anna had one thousand troops somewhere in Texas. Houston knew he did not have the men or supplies to fight multiple battles against a series of professional armies. He wanted a single, decisive battle. His best chance was to wait for the Mexicans to make a mistake from the frustration of chasing an enemy who wouldn't fight. Perhaps it was an old trick that he learned from living with the Cherokee Indians.

You won't find any footprints from Sam Houston along the Colorado River shoreline, but I bet he passed right by the live oak on the west side of the river pictured on the previous page. It is the second oldest live oak in Texas and is estimated to be five hundred years old. It was more than three hundred years old when Houston was here, and he must have noticed it.

Today, the campsite is Beason's Crossing Park in Columbus and a historical marker from 1936 commemorates the week that Houston spent there.

Getting There

COORDINATES FOR BEASON'S CROSSING PARK
29.705127871258046 / −96.53523224455242

COORDINATES FOR THE MEXICAN CAMP
29.705497592945353 / −96.56061242029162

COORDINATES FOR THE COLUMBUS OAK
29.70666492874792 / −96.55128281794202

10 CAMPING BY A SPRING

MARCH 26, 1836
NEAR MENTZ, TEXAS

WE KNOW that Sam Houston ordered one of his sudden retreats on the morning of March 26, 1836, soon after hearing of Fannin's defeat and capture. At the time of Houston's order, Fannin's four hundred men were still alive, but Houston knew he could no longer expect them to join his army at Beason's Crossing. Santa Anna's execution of the captives did not happen until the next day.

Now that Houston's army was around 1,400 men, it took a bit of time for the men to respond to his order. There was also a considerable amount of complaining about yet another retreat since they had been told to expect a battle soon. They eventually got moving around noon and burned Beason's buildings as they left.

Their campsite on that evening is a bit of a mystery and requires some detective work. There is no historical marker, but clues can be found in the memoirs of some of his soldiers. Each of these clues is insufficient on its own but taken together they point to a likely location near Mentz, Texas.

Here are the clues:

1. They went about six miles the first day.[1]
2. They went twenty miles to San Felipe the next day.[2]
3. They were going to San Felipe in a straight line.[3]
4. In order to travel quickly with perhaps 1,400 soldiers and numerous civilians, a road would have been preferable to going through undeveloped territory.
5. There was a spring or some water for the horses and men.[4]

Let's look at these historical pieces one at a time.

Evidence for the first hint comes from this passage written by Dr. N. D. Labadie, the French-Canadian doctor who tended the wounded at San Jacinto:

> We at once perceived that Houston had commenced his retreat. Before leaving that morning, it was hinted to me that a retreat was contemplated, notwithstanding the preparations apparently for a permanent encampment. I then, for the first time, addressed Gen. Houston on the subject, who knew me as well as I did him. He declared to me that the grass being all eaten up, and the horses starving, it was important to get a new and better range, and that, as there was a fine spring and plenty of grass six miles distant, he would only move to that place, and then camp.[5]

Evidence for the second clue comes from another soldier, J. H. Kuykendall, writing of the army's arrival at San Felipe, the next campsite: "A little after dark, having marched twenty miles, the army encamped on Spring creek—a mile and a half west of San Felipe."[6]

Taken together, these first two clues give us a combined distance of twenty-six miles from Beason's Crossing to the campsite at San Felipe, and this is just about exactly right if they went in a straight line as clue three suggests.

Information for the third piece comes from this passage in N. D. Labadie's account: "But Maj. Ben F. Smith, who knew everything that was transpiring, afterwards took me one side, and said with a wink: 'We are going to San Felipe, just as straight as the road will lead us—keep this to yourself.'"[7]

Support for the fourth clue can be found in the 1841 map of Colorado County (see below). The map indicates a road running through the Beason property that is marked "To San Felipe." It runs at a 60-degree angle to the north east. This road would probably have been the one that Houston took.

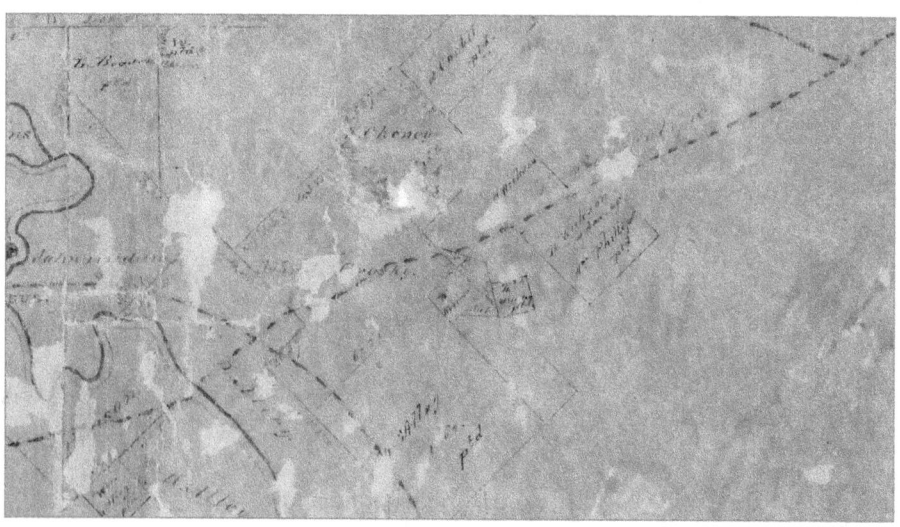

Horace L. Upshur, Colorado County, map, 1841, University of North Texas Libraries, The Portal to Texas History, found online at: *https://texashistory.unt.edu/ark:/67531/metapth88281/*.

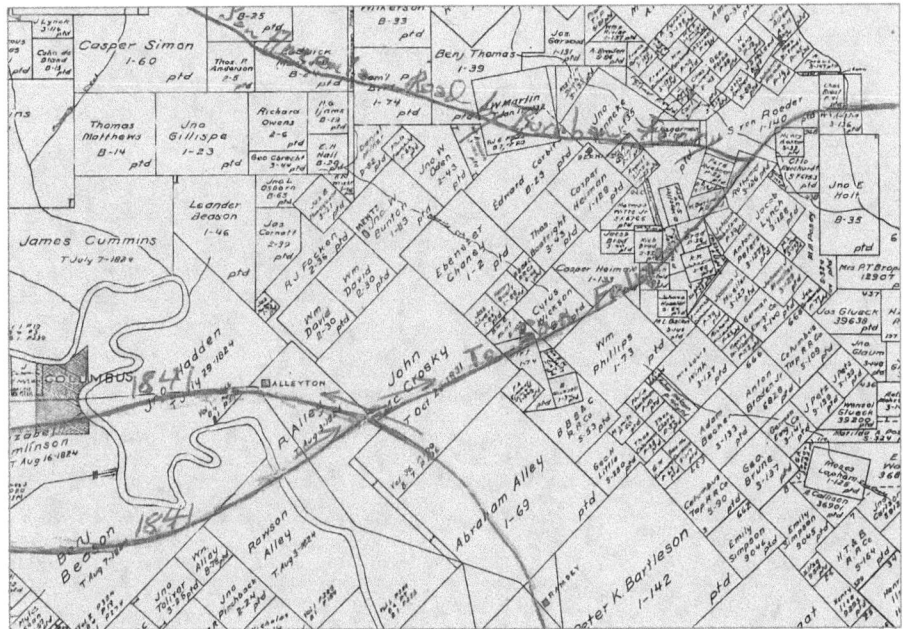

H. F. McDonald and J. Bascom Giles, Colorado County, map, 1920, University of North Texas Libraries, The Portal to Texas History, found online at: *https://texashistory.unt.edu/ark:/67531/metapth493653/*.

The same road is marked more clearly on a map from 1920 (see above).

If we put all five historical hints together, we come up with a six-mile line at about sixty degrees to the northeast from Beason's Crossing. This should be very close to the location of Houston's campsite on March 26.

If the March 26 location is accurate, it should be about twenty miles from the next campsite in San Felipe, and it is.

Finally, if we add in clue five, there should be a natural spring at this location. As mentioned previously, Labadie reports that Houston mentioned it, and later, Labadie saw the spring himself: "At near daybreak we came up with the army at the spring Gen. Houston had named to me."[8]

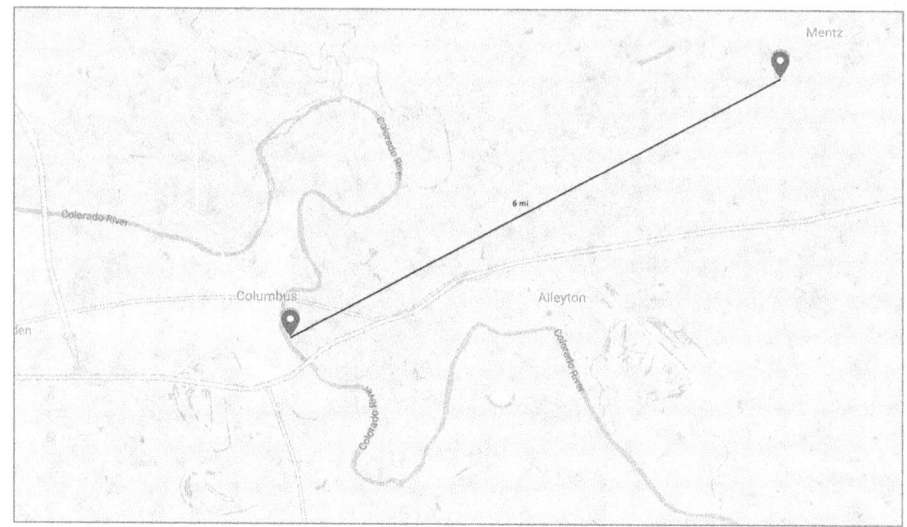

Google Maps.

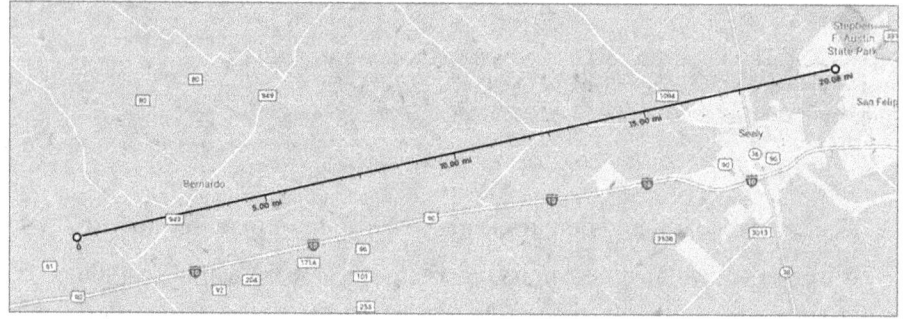

Google Maps.

US Geological Survey topographical map of the area.

Google Maps.

A United States Geological Survey (USGS) topographical map (top of page 57) confirms a swampy area at that location, a good sign of a spring.

Also, a satellite view from Google Maps (bottom of page 57) shows dark green vegetation around the swampy area as a sign of continuous dampness from a spring.

A visit to the site provides an enjoyable drive down Mentz Road, but no view of the potential campsite available due to dense foliage, as seen in the picture below. The site is on private property, so it is not accessible for a visit.

Getting There

COORDINATES FOR CAMP ON MENTZ ROAD
29.740502224076042 / −96.4491786630461

11 SAN FELIPE, THE POMPEII OF TEXAS

MARCH 27 AND 28, 1836
SAN FELIPE, TEXAS

THE RECOLLECTIONS of J. H. Kuykendall, one of Houston's soldiers, were first published in 1901 although they were probably written earlier. Kuykendall says that the army marched about twenty miles on March 27 and camped at a creek about one and a half miles west of San Felipe shortly after dark.[1] He gives the name of the creek as "Spring Creek," but there is no such name on present-day maps. There is, however, a creek that is, in part, exactly one and a half miles west of the historical center of San Felipe. Today, this creek is called Bullinger Creek. Since it is common for names to change over time, this may be the creek that Kuykendall referenced.

In addition, we know from another source that the camp at San Felipe was on the property of S. M. Williams.[2] Williams owned a lot of property in Texas, but an 1838 map (bottom of page 61) confirms that he owned land in the area along the creek near San Felipe.

Despite the open dissatisfaction among the soldiers, the army kept growing with new recruits. During the day, several of Fannin's soldiers caught up with the army and enlisted. They had been at the Battle of

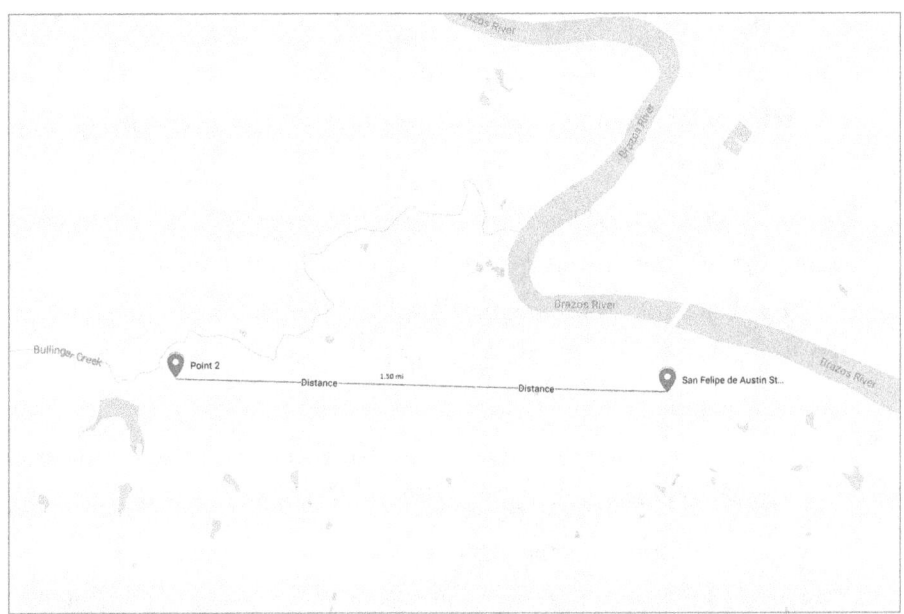

Google Maps.

Austin County, map, 1838, University of North Texas Libraries, The Portal to Texas History, found online at: *https://texashistory.unt.edu/ark:/67531/metapth88326/*.

The Road to San Jacinto

Coleto but, unlike the others, had avoided being captured. They did not know how lucky they were; on the day the men arrived (March 27, 1836), Fannin's other four hundred captured soldiers were executed at Goliad by the Mexicans.

The complaints of the soldiers finally boiled over into real mutiny, but Houston handled it well. When Houston left on the morning of March 28, two companies, one commanded by Moseley Baker and the other by Wyly Martin, refused to move out with the rest of the troops. There was no confrontation because Houston was already far ahead and on the way to his next camp when he found out. Baker, in particular, had been a vocal critic of Houston's strategy of retreating and Houston was pleased to have a good reason to remove him from contact with the rest of the army by giving him a valuable but remote assignment. Baker was assigned to cross the Brazos River at San Felipe and guard the crossing against the Mexican Army. Martin had a similar assignment down river at Fort Bend.

This worked out well because Baker and his forty men were able to hold off the much larger Mexican Army when they tried to cross. Baker's men endured several days of cannon fire while delaying the advance of the enemy. When the Mexicans eventually gave up and went to another location to cross, Baker pulled back and joined the rest of the army, feeling like a hero. He eventually participated in the Battle at San Jacinto where he was slightly wounded. The Mexican Army bypassed the crossing that Martin was defending so his assignment did not work out so well. He also retreated back to Houston's army but resigned prior to the battle.

Since Houston burned all the other towns as he left, one might expect him to burn San Felipe. But San Felipe was the original seat of Stephen F. Austin's colony in Texas, so burning it was of greater consequence than burning other locations. Houston left without burning San Felipe, but he did replenish his supply of coffee, sugar, bacon, shoes, and other necessities before he left, paying for them with a promissory note. But the story doesn't end there. San Felipe was burned shortly after Houston left Moseley Baker in charge of defending the crossing. Baker always claimed that Houston ordered him to burn it, but Houston denied doing so. If Houston did order Baker to burn San Felipe, it must have been a verbal order because Baker never produced any documentation of a written order. Contemporary politicians would say that Houston had plausible deniability. No matter who was right, it was a good tactic to deny any lodging or supplies to the enemy as the Mexican Army's supply lines grew longer.

One commentator thinks that it was burned when a scout mistook a distant herd of cattle for the approaching Mexican Army. Henry Stuart Foote, writing just five years after the events, states:

> On the evening of the 29th (March), some scouts, detached by Captain Baker, came in, saying, they had seen the Mexican advance guard, within a few miles of San Felipe, which place they would probably reach before daylight. This report was the cause of the Town being immediately set on fire and destroyed. It subsequently turned out, that this report of the scouts had originated in error, that they had mistaken a drove of cattle for a squadron of cavalry; and the Mexican troops did not in fact make their appearance near the Town till the 6th of April.[3]

Like Pompeii, San Felipe was destroyed all at once on a specific date; Pompeii in November 79 AD and San Jacinto on March 29, 1836. This is a big advantage to archaeologists because it provides some valuable

certainty and shows a snapshot of life at a specific moment. Of course, the fire at San Felipe did not preserve things quite as well as the volcanic ash of Pompeii.

The location for this site is on private property and not available for a visit, but you can drive down the same road that Houston probably used when he arrived. This is Esar Road on the west side of San Felipe.

COORDINATES FOR THE CAMP IN SAN FELIPE
29.805498737346145 / -96.1215890613063

12 MUDDY MILL CREEK

March 29, 1836
North of San Felipe

HOUSTON LEFT San Felipe with the goal of reaching Groce's Landing. As he had done previously, he moved his army to places where supporters lived and would provide food. The Groce family were wealthy cotton planters and slave owners who favored independence. To get to Groce's Landing, however, Houston had to lead his group through twenty miles of mud, flooded creeks, and heavy rain. They only made it three miles the first day, camping shortly after crossing Mill Creek.

The men, already complaining about the retreat, now had other sources of frustration: rain, mud, and sickness. They also had no other option than to keep moving. The army that once numbered 1,400 men had declined to perhaps five hundred, not including the two companies left behind to guard the Brazos River crossings. As a result of the difficult conditions, many soldiers were ill with ailments like measles, mumps, and flu, but one of them, Pvt. Felix G. Wright, became severely ill during this stretch of the journey on March 28. J. H. Kuykenedall wrote about the incident: "Next day (29th), in consequence of having to open a road through a thicket for our baggage wagons, we marched only three miles, and encamped about midway between Cummins's mill and Piney Creek. Here Wright died. Next morning (30th) we dug his grave in a little oak grove and having consigned him, uncoffined, to his dark abode, resumed the march."[1]

The long march in the mud must have been particularly joyless.

No cause of death was determined, but one commentator suggested cholera from drinking water contaminated with the cholera bacteria, though since everyone was drinking from the same water supply one would expect more cases.

Just a few days before, at Beason's Crossing, Wright had been healthy enough to volunteer for a special dangerous nighttime mission to guard an unguarded crossing of the Colorado River. Kuykendall documented the mission:

> Four miles farther down the river was the Atascocito crossing, which was unguarded. This circumstance, probably, did not occur to the general until late in the evening, about dusk, at which time he sent one of his aides to the camp of the company to which I belonged, with an urgent request that four or five of us would volunteer to proceed immediately down to said crossing. Felix G. Wright, David Lawrence, and myself, of Capt. McNutt's company; and John Ingram, of Capt. Hill's, at once volunteered for this service, and went to Gen. Houston's tent for his instruction. The general said, 'It is very dark, men, for which reason, footmen can more easily find their way down than horsemen. You will proceed silently and cautiously to the Atascocito crossing, where you will all remain until you are relieved tomorrow morning; unless the enemy shall present himself on the opposite side of the river, in which event one of you will mount your best horse and bring the news

as speedily as possible.' Guided by Ingram, we slowly and silently groped our way down to the crossing where we arrived about midnight. Here we remained until after sunrise the next morning without seeing or hearing aught of the enemy; and had already started back to camp when we met a relief guard of mounted men. About nine o'clock we got back to camp and reported to General Houston.[2]

Wright's loney grave and Houston's camp are still somewhere in the area shown in the 1860 map below. In honor of Private Wright, I visited the area of his death on a cold, rainy day. Somehow, it just seemed appropriate.

Austin County, map, 1860, University of North Texas Libraries, The Portal to Texas History, found online at: *https://texashistory.unt.edu/ark:/67531/metapth88327/*.

While not confirmed through primary sources, I think the Texas Army probably went north of San Felipe on a route that is now FM 331. I have no direct evidence for this assumption, but if they had gone a thousand feet to the left, the group would have needed to cross two creeks rather than one. If they had gone 3,600 feet to the right, they would also have needed to cross an additional creek. The scouts probably figured this out and sent them on the best path.

Of course, there is no way to know, but the location shown at the bottom of page 68 could have been where Houston's army crossed Mill Creek. The gently sloping banks would have been easy to climb. The location is next to the bridge on FM 331.

The grove of trees shown below, located about one mile north of Mill Creek, might be the final resting place of Pvt. Felix G. Wright. We may never know.

Getting There

COORDINATES FOR MILL CREEK
29.87023468649559 / -96.155660063381013

COORDINATES FOR POTENTIAL BURIAL SITE
29.8866471328639928 / -96.15014478168991

13 VICTORY OR DEATH AT RACCOON BEND

March 30, 1836
Raccoon Bend, Texas

EVEN THOUGH this was just a one-night campsite, something important happened at Raccoon Bend. Houston's men learned that surrender was not an option.

There is no marker for this site, but the following evidence identifies this location as a strong possibility:

1. William Zuber, one of Houston's men, stated that Houston was going to an area on the west side of the Brazos River, just across from property owned by Jared Groce, a wealthy supporter.
2. Both Zuber and J. H. Kuykendall state that the army marched seven or eight miles north after they buried Pvt. Felix G. Wright on the morning of March 30.[1]
3. As usual, even in the mud and rain, having a water source for the men and horses was a priority.
4. William Zuber provides a detailed account of thirty soldiers clearing a mile and a half road from this camp going east to the next camp.[2]

First, a march of almost nine miles would take Houston from the last camp site to the nearest water. Stopping at seven miles meant a site with no standing water. In the days before GPS, being a mile or so off on an estimate would not be unusual. The route identified on the map found on page 73 goes north from Private Wright's possible burial site along present-day FM 331.

Zuber's account of cutting a road though the vegetation to get to the next camp is fairly descriptive, particularly his note about working directly east. He states that thirty men were assigned:

> to cut a road a mile and a half long, going east through a dense bottom to a lake near the west bank of the Brazos, and to clear a camping ground for the army near the bank of the lake. If it had not been for an abandoned narrow road that lay through a continuous thicket of saplings, our detachment might have been occupied at least three days in cutting the road. But we worked to the lake in about four hours. Clearing the proposed camping ground was a laborious job, and we had to cut away and burn a great many wild grapevines . . .[3]

The small lake on the aerial map shown on page 74 is my suggestion for the location of this campsite. A trail going east to the next campsite at the larger lake would be 1.4 miles, roughly consistent with Zuber's account.[4]

The small lake did not show up on any of the old maps, raising some doubt that it was there in 1836. However, it is about five hundred feet long and probably too large to be a recently man-made stock pond. It was probably just a detail that was considered to be too insignificant for inclusion. The larger lake to the right was also normally left off.

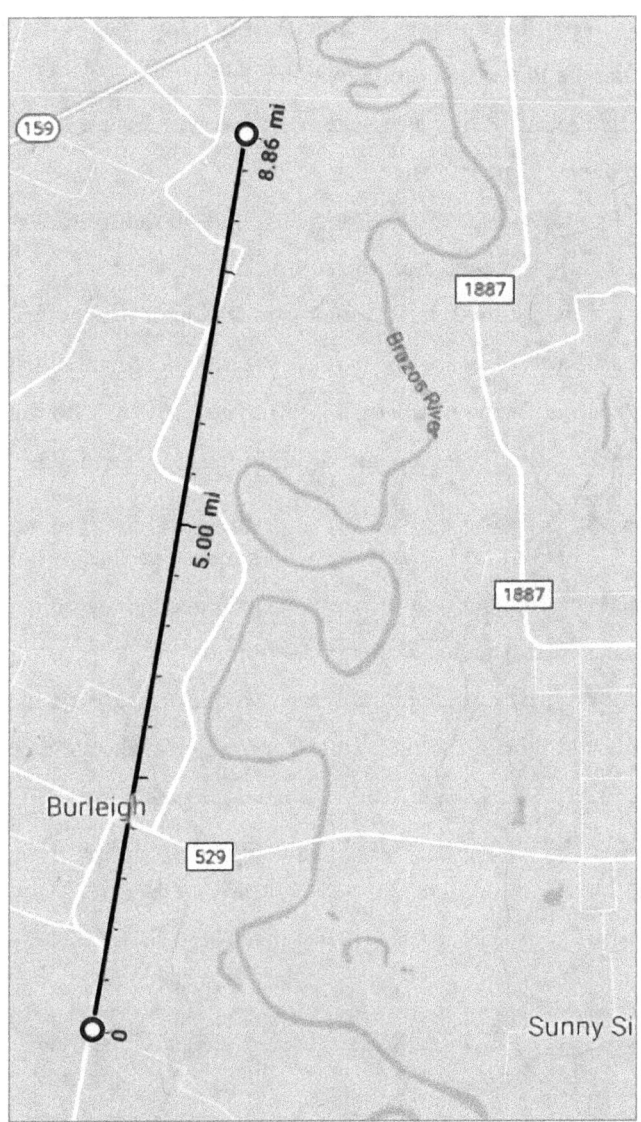

Google Maps.

There is some other information that is inconsistent. Zuber said they camped at Foster's Plantation and Kuykendall said they camped at Bracey's.[5] Neither name shows up on the old maps of Austin County, so it seems that this evidence is inconclusive.

A visit to this area takes you to the Raccoon Bend oil field. Oil was discovered in this location in 1928 and it is still producing eight hundred barrels per day. It is expected to keep producing for the next twenty-five years. Raccoon Bend is probably not on anyone's vacation destination list, but I went there for a look at the campsite. Unfortunately, the road to the small lake had a locked gate that prevented me from getting too close. Below is a view of the possible campsite from that locked gate.

I wanted to see if I could find any of the wild grapevines that Zuber had to cut through. When I looked to the right of the fence I saw a tangle of vines that may be similar to what Zuber encountered.

The area may look a little desolate now, but on March 30, 1836, it must have looked wonderful to the six soldiers from Fannin's unit who showed up unexpectedly. They had escaped the Goliad Massacre by playing dead and jumping in the river while more than four hundred soldiers were slaughtered. These six soldiers had been on the run for three days. This is how Houston's army found out that Santa Anna had done the

unthinkable: mass murder of unarmed prisoners. Some of the Mexican soldiers could not bring themselves to fire their guns and this probably helped with the six men's escape.

The famous victory or death letter that commander Travis wrote from the Alamo on February 24 now had more meaning to Houston's men. Surrender would mean execution. There was another option to consider, however—retreat across the Sabine River to the safety of the United States. Increasingly, the Texan soldiers were worried that Houston was going to take this third option.

COORDINATES FOR POSSIBLE CAMPSITE
30.01568547746856 / -96.1298534257422

14 BASIC TRAINING ON THE BRAZOS RIVER

March 31 to April 12, 1836
Near Raccoon Bend, Texas

UNMARKED DIRT ROADS, mud, loose dogs, and a no trespassing sign. No wonder few people have seen this site. Starbucks? Don't even ask; the nearest one is more than a thirty-mile drive.

Around Raccoon Bend, Sam Houston formed a basic training camp for an army of untrained, poorly equipped amateurs. Discipline was the goal—no music, no liquor, and no card games were allowed. Houston knew that these soldiers would either win against a larger, more experienced, better-equipped army or be dead soon. And all of them would be dead, as happened at the Alamo and Goliad. Houston did not care if his men liked him or not; he did not need to worry about popularity. He also knew the Mexican Army was looking for them.

Houston could not afford a pitched battle trying to defend a fixed location, much like the situation at the Alamo. Allowing a small army to be surrounded by a larger force would mean certain failure. Mobility was his advantage, and he knew he had to out maneuver the bigger force that was chasing him. Houston wanted to frustrate the Mexican Army, and

hoped they would make a mistake. He figured his rag-tag bunch of angry volunteers might be good for one decisive battle, but no more.

Strategically, this camp was in a good defensive position on the west bank of the Brazos River, where both of his flanks and his rear were guarded by the river. Water was available and Jared Groce, a wealthy supporter, was just across the river as a source of supplies. If Houston needed to move the army quickly, the steamboat *Yellowstone* was docked and available. The only potential approach for the enemy was from the front, through mud and tangled vines. For an army on the run, the situation was about as good as it would get—safety, water, supplies, and no marching.

There were still lots of things for the men to complain about, however. It rained frequently in the two weeks they were at the site. Soldiers trained in mud that was sometimes knee-deep. Many wore deer skin moccasins that shrank when they got wet. Rations consisted of an ear of corn per day for each man and sometimes a little beef. They drank stagnant water from on old branch of the river that was now landlocked. Guard duty in the rain could last for twenty-four hours.

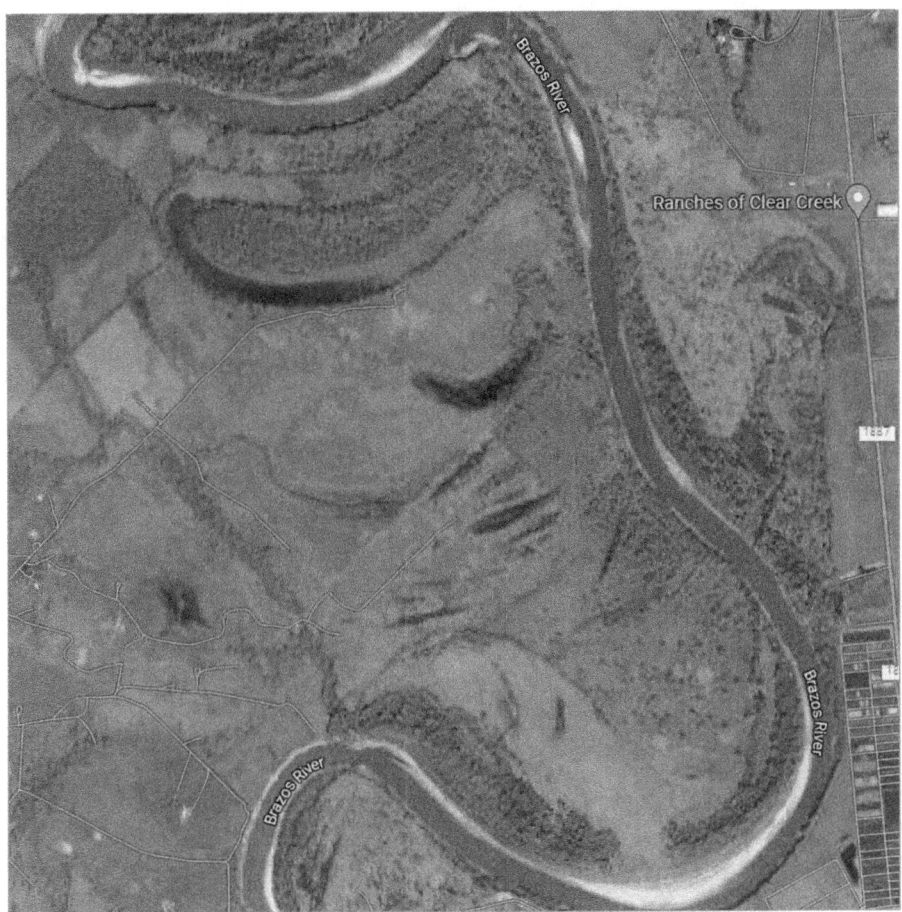
Google Maps satellite view of the camp.

It's no wonder that some of the soldiers wanted out. Pvt. Abraham Scales was charged with desertion and mutiny; Pvt. John Garner was charged with desertion and disobedience. Both were convicted and sentenced to be shot the next day. Houston quickly pardoned popular young Scales (who vanished again in a week, this time permanently) but most agreed that Garner was a real villain who they could do without.[1]

John Garner's execution was scheduled for noon on April 3, 1836, Easter Sunday. The entire army stood in a semi-circle to watch. Many present had never seen another man shot to death at close range, so emotions ran high. A grave was dug, and Garner was kneeling in front of his coffin with the firing squad almost ready to fire when Col. George Washington Hockley showed up with clemency orders from Houston. Garner staggered to his feet looking dazed.

Houston had made his point and, perhaps, he thought he just might need a villain in his army—he was right. Garner went on to distinguish himself at San Jacinto and was one of the volunteers who destroyed the bridge over Vince's Bayou.

While at this camp, the distrust of Houston's leadership finally reached the executive level of the new government. Interim President of Texas David Burnet ordered Houston to stop retreating and fight. Houston and Burnet were natural opponents. The two things that Burnet hated most were drinking and cursing—Houston was accomplished at both, although he gave up drinking during the military campaign. Burnet finally sent Secretary of War Tom Rusk to join the army with the authority to take command if Houston continued to retreat.[2] Houston confided his strategy to Rusk, and Rusk soon became a supporter rather than a replacement.

Getting There

COORDINATES FOR THE CAMP ON THE BRAZOS
30.009338175594472 / -96.1149198266859

15 SAM HOUSTON MEETS THE TWIN SISTERS

April 12, 1836
South of Hempstead, Texas

NO ACCOUNT of the Texas Revolution would be complete without some discussion of the Twin Sisters, the two cannon that were donated by the people of Cincinnati, Ohio. They were small artillery pieces that probably shot a 6 lb. cannonball, although some sources say the cannonball size was only 4 lb. In any case, Sam Houston mainly shot broken pieces of horseshoes, bent nails, and used bullets because he was short on ammunition and these materials produced a shotgun effect that was best used against soldiers. Most discussions of the Twin Sisters cover their role in the battle and the futile search for the missing pieces throughout the last decades. In order to fill out the story of the Twin Sisters, however, let's visit the exact location where Sam Houston first met the two cannon.

The artillery pieces were named the Twin Sisters because a set of twins, young ladies, brought them down the Mississippi River by boat. Someone thought it would be charming to make these young ladies part of the welcoming ceremony for the cannon and it must have been a good idea because the name stuck.

Why was Cincinnati interested in supporting the Texas Revolution? First, Capt. Sidney Sherman's company, the "Kentucky Riflemen," was from Newport, Kentucky, near Cincinnati. Second, Cincinnati was first settled by many soldiers from George Washington's army. They named it "Cincinnati" in honor of the Roman general Cincinnatus who turned down an offer to remain as dictator after a victory and went back home to his farm. He exchanged his sword for a plough in an act that displayed civic virtue. George Washington turned down a similar offer and the people of Cincinnati thought they saw these qualities of character in Sam Houston. They wanted to reward that concept of the citizen-soldier.

When Houston first heard of the Twin Sisters, he knew immediately that they would provide a big confidence boost to his army. His men were mostly armed with hunting weapons from home and the army possessed no artillery. With few advantages other than attitude, they were getting ready to face a larger professional army. The Twin Sisters were immediately loved by the soldiers, though soldiers soon started to complain about pulling them through the mud.

The Twin Sisters came down the Mississippi River to New Orleans on a steamboat then traveled overland to Brazoria and then Galveston where their progress was delayed by conflicting orders and military confusion. Houston worried that the cannon might get lost in the confusion, so he sent Maj. Leander Smith to look after them. Smith found the pieces in Harrisburg, about fifty miles from Houston's encampment near Raccoon Bend, and left to return to Houston's army with the cannon on April 9.[1] Since there was no water route, Smith used a horse and cart to bring the artillery pieces to Houston by traveling the old Harrisburg Road. Smith reached Groce's Plantation home—named Bernado—on April 12. The house was about four miles south of present-day Hempstead and on a bluff overlooking the river.

This is where Houston first met the Twin Sisters, on April 12 after crossing the Brazos River on the steamboat *Yellowstone*. The *Yellowstone* was in the area to move cotton to market for Jared Groce's plantation, but Houston was allowed to use it for the army. It took several trips to transport the army and all the animals to the east side of the river. The Twin Sisters were waiting for him in front of Groce's home, Bernado, on the east side of the Brazos River. Houston had already ordered a field hospital be built at the site, and many soldiers were already there.[2]

It seems like the soldiers would be eager to test fire the Twin Sisters, but two factors prevented the demonstration. First, the Texans had only a small amount of gunpowder and they wanted to save it for the battle. There should have been little concern about them actually working since their design was simple: a single piece of iron with no moving parts. The

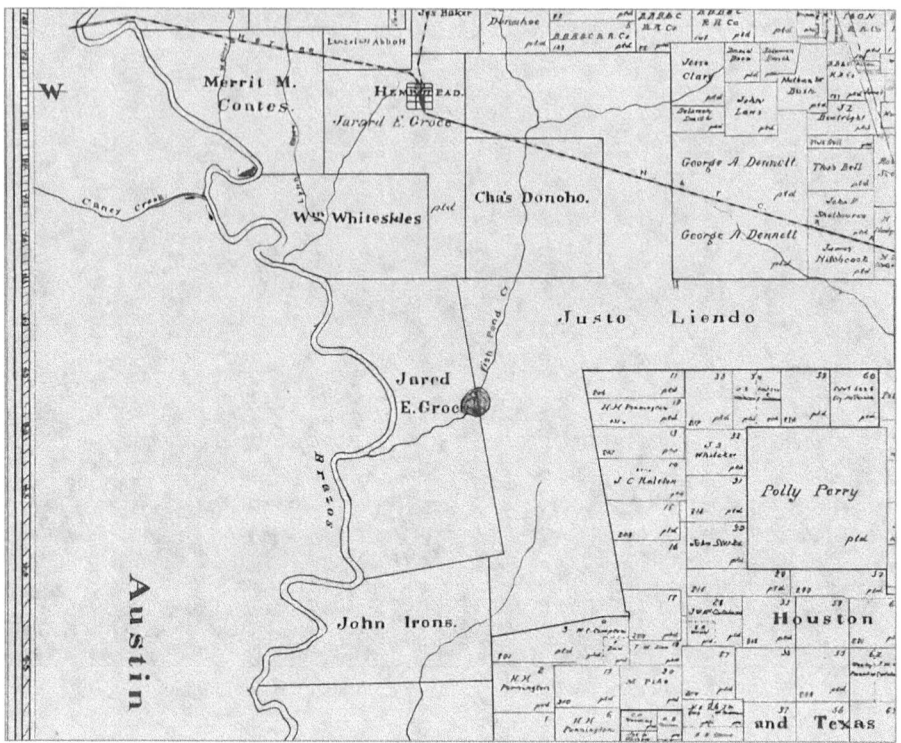

Herman Pressler and J. W. Morris, Waller County, map, 1900, University of North Texas Libraries, The Portal to Texas History, found online at: *https://texashistory.unt.edu/ark:/67531/metapth492985/*.

first shot fired by the Twin Sisters was at San Jacinto during the opening skirmish against Santa Anna's big cannon, the Golden Standard. The Golden Standard's opening shot was high and into the trees, but the Twin Sisters were on target. Unfortunately, the first casualty was the hapless mule pulling the Golden Standard.

Second, the artillery pieces were not mounted on a supporting structure, so the cannon were not ready to use. Houston's men stayed up all night building wooden carriages for them. The wheels for the carriages were probably taken from some existing wagon because it would be difficult to build a new wheel from scratch.

The exact location where Houston first met the Twin Sisters is about four miles south of Hempstead on FM 1887. Since 1992, Creekside Nursey has used the location to raise trees and plants. Sam Houston, and the people of Cincinnati, would be pleased to know that the location had returned to peaceful uses. In the spirit of Cincinnatus, the weapons of war have been exchanged for the implements of agriculture.

NOTE: *Traveling south on FM 1887 is a historical marker on the right. This marker, erected in 1936, is best ignored because it contains an error—it claims to mark the location of Houston's camp, but the camp was actually on the west side of the river.*

Getting There

COORDINATES FOR HOUSTON MEETING THE TWIN SISTERS
30.006544855249615 / -96.0820913959978

16 RENDEZVOUS AT DONOHO'S PLANTATION

April 14, 1836
South of Hempstead, Texas

THE TEXAS ARMY was on the move after two weeks of training in the muddy campground on the west side of the Brazos River. The men were still poorly armed and poorly clothed, but spirits were improving with prospects for battle with Santa Anna's forces. Of course, there was still pervasive doubt about Houston's intentions. Many soldiers thought he was taking them over the border into the safety of United States territory and there was grumbling about replacing him.

The march from Groce's Plantation to Donoho's Plantation was a brief three miles, a nice change from the fifteen to twenty miles per day they had previously traveled. Sam Houston wanted to bring all his troops together in one place for the next leg of the journey. Some soldiers were stationed at Washington-on-the-Brazos, others guarded the east bank of the Brazos River opposite San Felipe, and some came from Fort Bend. Donoho's looked like a good rendezvous point, except for one thing: Houston neglected to tell Charles Donoho about the plan.

Houston's army had been warmly received by Jared Groce because the two men knew each other in advance. Groce made his property available

for the field hospital and opened his home to civilian refugees. Houston probably expected a similar reception at Donoho's, but soon found out that Donoho did not support the revolution. With Donoho's position, it's no wonder he became upset when the uninvited guests started cutting down his trees and using his fencing for firewood. He was outnumbered perhaps a thousand to one, however, so he abandoned his property. That was when the real party started. There was music and dancing into the evening and some of the nearby refugee women joined in the fun.

The site is currently The John Fairey Garden (formerly Peckerwood Garden). It contains thirty-nine acres of exotic plants from Mexico and Asia that were collected over a lifetime by the recently deceased owner, John Fairey. It is open to the public and well worth a visit on its own merits apart from the history.

There is a small spring-fed stream which was probably the water supply for the plantation. You can bet that Sam Houston watered his two hundred horses right here.

Records indicate that there should be a historical marker for this site, but no one has seen it in years. According to state documents it was located four miles southeast of Hempstead, on the west side of FM 359 and north of FM 3346. The marker was installed in 1936 as part of the centennial celebration. The huge granite rocks that the markers consist of don't vanish easily, so we're left with wondering, what happened? After some on-site research revealed nothing, I moved the investigation online. The website for the Waller County Historical Society has a map that locates the marker a bit to the north of the John Fairy Garden. In an email exchange, a representative from the historical society informed me that the marker was placed on private property and the property owner does not allow visitors. I subsequently learned that markers from that time were sometimes placed on private property without securing any access rights, so there is no legal remedy available. But the John Fairey Garden next door is open to the public and would welcome visitors motivated by history.

NOTES: *Special thanks to Junior McKay of the Waller County Historical Society and Louis Aulbach of the Houston Archaeological Society for helping me research this site.*

COORDINATES FOR DONOHO'S
30.05646534469944 / -96.03813237950045

17 McCarley's Home

April 15, 1836
North of Hockley, Texas

SAM HOUSTON'S MEN seized some cattle here on April 15, 1836. Samuel McCarley and his ten children had evacuated in front of Santa Anna's approaching army so nobody was around to complain. Even if they had been there, standing up to more than a thousand hungry soldiers would have been intimidating, and the family most likely would have relented. The soldiers took everything they could find to eat and tore down McCarley's fence to build the fire to cook their dinner.

The mood among the soldiers was not good. They had marched twenty miles in a cold rain and had to lug the Twin Sisters through the mud. The soldiers were eager to get the two iron cannon donated by the people of Cincinnati, but when the artillery finally arrived the men had to face the reality of the Twin Sisters' weight. Even with a pair of borrowed oxen pulling them, the pieces slowed down the pace of the army and became just something else to complain about. Also, at this point, they had been retreating for about a month and they worried that their leader did not want to fight the enemy. They knew they were only three miles

away from a well-known fork in the road that would force a decision to either fight or continue retreating. Mutiny was in the air.

After the feast on fresh beef, the soldiers camped at this site. The small hill pictured above probably was not there then; it must have been built by the developer to form a boundary between the development and the road. Since sources describe the use of fence posts for fuel to build fire, the fence in the picture was obviously built after 1836.

Apparently, the McCarley family did complain about the confiscated beef after the war because in 1858, twenty-two years later, McCarley's widow was reimbursed $460 by the State of Texas, by then a part of the United States.[1] It seems it has always been hard to get a refund from the government!

COORDINATES FOR McCARLEY HOMESTEAD
30.0696556763030168 / −95.8070691337430

18 FORK IN THE ROAD

April 16, 1836
New Kentucky Park, Texas

SAM HOUSTON'S MEN woke up on April 16, 1836, knowing that a decision would have to be made after a short three-mile march down this road. The left fork would take to army to Nacogdoches and eventually to the safety of the United States. That option might also result in mutiny from the soldiers who wanted to fight. The right fork went to Harrisburg where Santa Anna was known to be headed.

Houston did not reveal the plans to his men. Some still say it is because he had not made up his mind, but I think his flair for the dramatic (as shown in the execution that was stopped at the last moment) was designed to get his men to display maximum commitment. Besides, there was some risk, and little reward, in letting every one of his inexperienced soldiers know too much. For example, if one of the men were captured by Santa Anna, he would probably give up information under interrogation. As a matter of fact, that did happen back on April 7, but it worked to Houston's advantage. The captured soldier told the Mexicans that the government had moved to Harrisburg (which was true) and that Houston's army was headed for Nacogdoches and probably Louisiana (which the soldier

thought to be true).[1] Santa Anna acted on this faulty information and decided to pursue the government rather than the army. Perhaps this was exactly the mistake that Houston had been waiting for. The frustrated Sana Anna risked all for a quick checkmate.

As the army approached the fork, the soldiers at the front of the line asked the local landowner, Abraham Roberts, which fork would go to Harrisburg. He directed them to the right and they immediately started down that path with a cheer and a song. The decision was made. They were going after Santa Anna. It may be important to note that Sam Houston seems to have not been at the front of the marching army. Perhaps that is evidence that he wanted the men to make the decision and feel committed to it.

N. D. Labadie, a French-Canadian physician who joined the Texan Army, describes the moment:

> Owing to the conflicting opinions as to which road the army was to take after reaching Mr. Roberts, where it forked, I wanted to satisfy myself on that point, and went to Maj. Ben Smith, for information. He replied to my inquiry that it was his opinion the army would continue straight on and cross the Trinity at Robbins' Ferry. As many were unwilling to go on that road, a halt was expected to be made at Roberts', and as we reached that point (17th April) the writer, with three or four others, galloped to near the advance guard, the Captain of which told us he had received no orders but would go between the two roads. As Gen. Houston was now coming up, several of us desired Mr. Roberts, who was standing on his gate, to point out to all—*the road to Harrisburgh* [sic]. Gen. Houston was then close by, and when Roberts raised his hand, and elevating his voice, cried out: "The right hand road will carry you to Harrisburg just as straight as a compass." A shout was then raised: "To the right boys, to the right." The whole line was fast closing up, as the music stopped; but upon hearing the shout of the men, the music proceeded to the right.[2]

While Labadie seems to have gotten the date wrong (this transpired on April 16, not April 17), the recounting provides a glimpse into the exact moment Houston's men finally decided to trust their leader.

That spot today is in a quiet wooded park in the New Kentucky Park subdivision. The developers must have understood the historical significance of the area because many of the street names are dripping with history: Decision Drive, Musket Run, Marksman Court, Victorious Drive, etc. How would you like to grow up at the corner of Fearless and Courageous?

The park has lots of tall pines and one huge old live oak tree that has been woven into the story because it would be really cool if it were true. Some people tell the story with one of the tree's branches pointing to the Harrisburg route; others have Houston making his decision while sitting under the tree. While we know what really happened because of Labadie's account, it is still a beautiful tree, and since live oaks can live

for five hundred years or more, the tree was almost certainly there when Houston passed by.

Of course, there was one problem as a result of the decision to fight: Houston's army lost the borrowed oxen that were pulling the Twin Sisters cannon. A feisty widow named Pamelia Mann lent her oxen on the promise that they were going to safety, not into battle. She disrupted the march, cut the oxen free with her knife, and took them with her. Even Sam Houston was speechless and intimidated by a well-armed Texas woman. After reading how Noah Smithwick, one of Houston's soldiers, tells the story, one might well see Pamelia Mann as the archetypal tough Texas woman:

> When the army was in retreat to San Jacinto, General Houston issued an order for work oxen to be taken wher ever [sic] found. Rohrer—" General" Rohrer the boys called him—took a yoke of cattle belonging to an old woman Mrs. M.—who had a farm on the Brazos. The teams were all hitched up ready to start, when up rode Madame with knife and pistol belted on.
>
> Spurring up to Rohrer she commanded him to unhitch her oxen. Rohrer referred her to General Houston. The General being pointed out to her, the old woman rode up to him and demanded her property. Houston attempted to explain the exigencies of the case, but the Amazon swore she would have them, emphasizing her determination with oaths that took all the wind out of the General's sail, though he was accounted a proficient in the art of swearing. Throwing up his hands he exclaimed: "Take them, my dear woman, take them. For God Almighty's sake take them." Back she went to Rohrer, and, upon his refusal to unhitch the

cattle, herself dismounted and released them, retiring in triumph, having vanquished both General Houston and General Rohrer, the only time either of them was ever whipped.[3]

COORDINATES FOR WHICH WAY TREE
30.079515774110728 / −95.76075300723136

19 TELGE PARK, THE CAPITOL OF TEXAS (FOR A DAY)

April 16, 1836
Near Cypress, Texas

PUT YOURSELF in Sam Houston's shoes. He had just spent two tough weeks living in the mud at his training camp at the Brazos River. He knew many of his men hated him and some were plotting to replace him. Many had deserted. Others thought he was afraid to fight Santa Anna and was going to retreat all the way to the Louisiana border. Then around noon on April 16, 1836, his soldiers found out that Houston was going to take them to Harrisburg to fight the Mexicans. They were ecstatic, and the next twenty miles passed with his soldiers singing and joking. Houston must have felt relieved. His men no longer thought he was a coward, the plan was set and everyone was eager. Houston must have still been worried that the coming battle would not be quick and easy as his joyful, inexperienced men thought—it turns out he was wrong about that.

When the Texas Army came to a stopping place at Burnett's Plantation they found the house empty but Burnett had left his cattle and chickens. The hungry men saw an opportunity for a barbeque, and they used

Burnett's fence for firewood as they had done previously. The difference here was the chickens. The men had eaten nothing for days but beef on a stick roasted over an open fire. Worse yet, they had no salt. Unfortunately, they had been told not molest the chickens or use any of Burnett's personal property.

The thought of a chicken dinner was too tempting for S. F. Sparks, one of Houston's soldiers. He recalled that chicken dinner all his life, describing it in his recollections published in 1908:

> It was strictly against orders to kill a hog or chickens or anything except beef. We arrived at Burnett's at about two or three o'clock in the afternoon. We found that the family had all left the place, and that there was a yard full of chickens, plenty of corn meal, and bacon in the smoke-house, besides pots and ovens.

> I went to work and killed twelve grown chickens, dressed them, and put them in a large wash pot; I also put in some sliced bacon. I then made an oven and a large skillet of cornbread. I took six of the chickens, and put them in a dinner pot, with at least half a gallon of rich gravy, and set it away, together with the oven of bread.
>
> The yard was covered with feathers, and the men said to me, "Ain't you afraid Houston will punish your [sic] if you don't take those feathers away?" I said, "No." Well, we all did justice to that dinner.

Later that evening, Houston arrived with some other officers. The feathers told the story, so Sparks recalled:

> I saw Houston knit his brows when he saw the feathers in the yard. . . . I addressed Houston in the following way, "General, I have disobeyed orders; when we arrived here, I found everything deserted and we were hungry, for we have had nothing to eat, except beef; so I killed some chickens and baked some bread, and we had a good dinner!" He looked at me as if he were looking through me, and said, "Sparks, I will have to punish you. You knew it as against orders; I will have to punish you."
>
> I said, "General, I saved you some," and I took the lids off the vessels that contained the chicken and the bread, and told them to help themselves . . . Rusk said, "General, if you don't come on we'll eat all the dinner. We have not had such a dinner since we left home. Sparks is a good cook."
>
> Then the General drew his knife, and attacked the dinner . . . After the meal, General Houston said, "Sparks, I'll not punish you

for this offense, but if you are guilty of it a second time, I will double the punishment."[1]

The site of Burnett's plantation is known today as Telge Park and it looks like a normal suburban park. You won't find any chicken feathers, but if you follow the trail back to the creek, it probably looks much like it did when Sam Houston left his footprints here.

Burnett's was a regular stopping point along the road to Harrisburg. The interim government of Texas stayed here on March 22, 1836, while evacuating to Harrisburg. One might say this spot was the capitol of Texas for one day. Wouldn't it be nice for the local Chamber of Commerce to schedule a "Capitol of Texas (for a Day) Day," where folks could hold a chicken eating contest in memory of all of the Burnett chickens that Houston's men ate? Seems like something Houston would have enjoyed.

The Road to San Jacinto

 **Getting There**

COORDINATES FOR TELGE PARK
29.95405493251514 / -95.647920826 93336

20 WHERE DID SAM HOUSTON'S ARMY CAMP ON APRIL 17, 1836?

April 17, 1836
Houston, Texas

THERE IS NO historical marker for this site because nobody really knows where Sam Houston camped on the evening of April 17, 1836. It is probably somewhere in the present-day Houston city limits, but there is no agreement on the exact location. Residents of the upscale Woodland Heights area have been eager to claim that the location was in their neighborhood and I bet some prospective homebuyers have been told that Sam Houston may have camped in the back yard of the home they are considering. I have a different suggestion.

This will give you a chance to do a bit of detective work with me. Some of Sam Houston's soldiers published their recollections after the war and I have tried to find some hints in them. Here are a few details that may help locate the site:

1. Houston was trying to reach Harrisburg before Santa Anna got there.
2. The army travelled fifteen miles that day from the prior camp at Burnett's homesite.[1]

3. The camp was about six miles north of Harrisburg.[2]
4. The camp was at the edge of a pine forest.[3]
5. The camp was at the head of a bayou.[4]

Can these all be woven consistently into an argument for a location?

Let's first examine number one, which is true but misleading. Although Houston wanted to reach Harrisburg, he actually chose not to visit. On the evening of April 18, he camped north of Buffalo Bayou in the Galena Park area. Harrisburg was south of the bayou (near the intersection of Broadway and Lawndale in Houston's present-day East End). From the north side of the bayou, Houston could see that Harrisburg had been destroyed and was on fire, so there was no point in crossing the bayou especially since it was swollen from the recent rain. This changes the course of the Texas Army to the east away from present-day Woodland Heights area a bit.[5]

Next, the distance estimates in points two and three must contain an error. If Houston and his men travelled fifteen miles and had six more miles to go, the total distance from his camp at Burnett's homesite to their destination on April 18 should be twenty-one miles. However, the actual distance, according to Google Maps, is approximately twenty-eight miles. Therefore, the estimates are off by seven miles and can't prove any precise location. Since we know the army arrived at its destination around noon on April 18, they could not have camped much more than six miles away. Given that Houston's men had to drag the Twin Sisters through muddy terrain without the aid of a team of oxen, the army probably traveled about two miles per hour at best. Anything more that eight or ten miles would be hard to reconcile with a noon arrival on April 18.[6]

What about points four and five? Are there any potential sites within a reasonable distance range that meet these criteria?

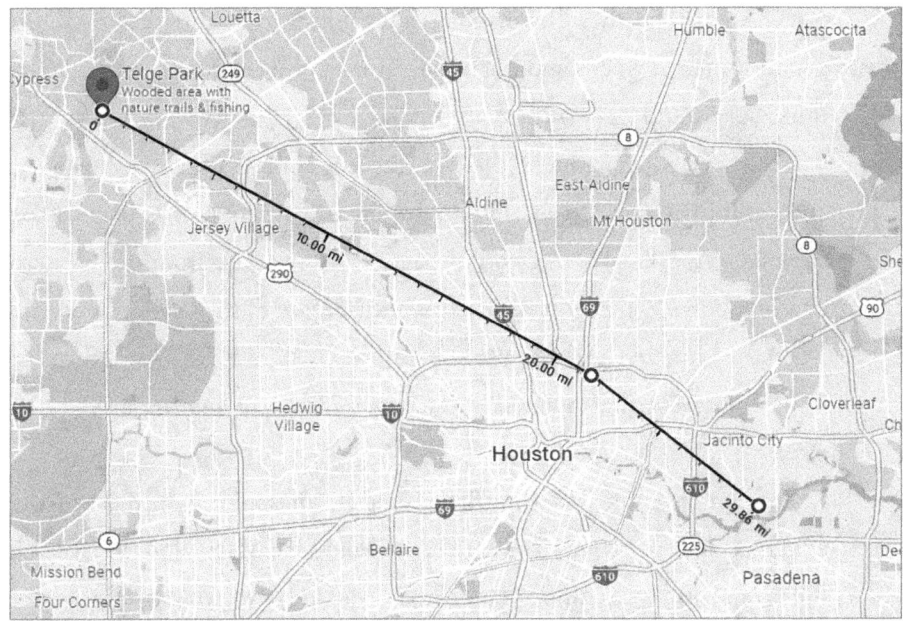

Google Maps.

The Texas Piney Woods is a huge pine forest that covers much of East Texas. The boundaries have changed over the years, especially when much of it was harvested for timber, but its present-day southern border reaches almost all the way to the North Loop in northeast Houston as shown in the Google Map above. This may have been the pine forest that the troops recall. It may have been more extensive when Sam Houston was here, but this would be a good place to look for a bayou that Sam Houston may have camped on.

Is there a bayou that has its head in this general area? It appears that Hunting Bayou is the only bayou that has headwaters in this area. From its headwaters near the North Loop just east of the Hardy Toll Road, Hunting Bayou runs southeast into Buffalo Bayou near where Houston's army camped on April 18. It might have been a natural guide to their next camp.

The actual headwaters, shown in a present-day picture (below), is just a muddy area of weeds and might not have been a good campground for a thirsty army and its horses.

However, about a mile to the east, there is enough water for the horses and would still be easy for an army to cross. Perhaps this is where they camped. The photo at the top of page 109 was taken from the western end of George Street just inside the intersection of the North Loop and I-69 in Kashmere Gardens.

If more water was needed, the bayou widens out another mile to the east.

In summary, the Hunting Bayou site is consistent with most of the evidence stated above. Houston's army would have travelled twenty-one miles on April 17 to camp at Hunting Bayou and then another eight miles on April 18 to reach the location in Galena Park by noon. The edge of the pine forest is provided by the Texas Piney Woods which may have been

closer than it is now. Hunting Bayou is the only bayou in that area to have its headwaters nearby. Of course, this is still speculation, but it is based on some evidence.

It looks like Kashmere Gardens seems to have a better claim for being Sam Houston's camp site on April 17, 1836, than Woodland Heights.

NOTE: *Many thanks to Louis Aulbach for suggesting Hunting Bayou.*

Getting There

COORDINATES FOR CAMPSITE ON APRIL 17
29.806405049598446 / −95.33245481026633

21 CAMP NEAR HARRISBURG

April 18–19, 1836
Galena Park, Texas

HOUSTON'S ARMY reached this spot on the north side of Buffalo Bayou around noon on April 18, 1836, after a seven-mile march from the previous camp. The site is now in Galena Park, a heavily industrialized area. Initially, the Texans intended to cross the Buffalo Bayou to go to Harrisburg, but there were two problems with that idea. First, they needed to figure out how to get the army to the other side; Buffalo Bayou was approximately two hundred yards wide and too deep to wade. Second, there was no need to visit Harrisburg because they could see the smoke rising from the ruins on the other side of the bayou. Santa Anna had burned the town the day before while trying to capture the Texas government officials.

The army still needed to cross the bayou to intercept Santa Anna at Lynch's Ferry which controlled the main route east. Houston found an old leaky ferry boat that his men repaired by removing the floorboards from the nearby home of Isaac Batterson. According to one soldier, the boat was so small that it could only hold twelve people at a time.[1] Batterson got an historical marker out of the deal, and the site of that home is now the

Galena Park City Hall. This is also the site where Houston left his baggage and supplies during the battle. There were 248 soldiers left here as guards although most were too sick from measles or the flu to participate in the battle. He tried to convince Juan Seguín and his group of Tejano soldiers to stay since he was afraid they would be confused with Mexican soldiers during the battle, but they were too eager to fight. Just to be safe, the men put pieces of cardboard in their hats to identify themselves, although the precaution turned out to be unnecessary. Houston also considered leaving the Twin Sisters here but was argued out of that position. It turned out that bringing the cannon still further was a good decision since the artillery pieces played an important part in winning the battle.

At this spot, Houston wrote a short letter to the people of Texas announcing the upcoming battle:

TO THE PEOPLE OF TEXAS

April 19, 1836

We view ourselves on the eve of battle. We are nerved for the conquest, and must conquer or perish. It is vain to look for present aid: None is at hand. We must now act or abandon all hope! Rally to the standard. And be no longer the scoff of mercenary tongues! Be men, be freemen, that your children may bless their fathers' names! Colonel Rusk is with me and I am rejoiced at it. The country will be the gainer, and myself the beneficiary. Liberty and our country!

Sam Houston, Commander-in-Chief[2]

Houston also gave a rousing speech on horseback to the entire army that ended with everyone cheering, "Remember the Alamo." Dr. Labadie provides an eyewitness account:

Before crossing the Bayou, Gen. Houston made us an animated speech, towards the conclusion of which he said: "The army will cross and we will meet the enemy. Some of us may be killed and must be killed; but, soldiers, remember the Alamo, the Alamo! The Alamo!" Maj. Somerville remarked: "After such a speech, but d—d few will be taken prisoners—that I know."[3]

A few days ago, Houston's men hated him; now they were ready to risk their lives and follow him into battle.

After the speech, the Texans crossed Buffalo Bayou between Sim's Bayou and Vince's Bayou by using the repaired ferry boat in a series of trips that took all day. Houston's army would have taken the path pictured

Camp Near Harrisburg

at the top of page 114 to reach the bayou from the Batterson house. That walk today would take you by a flour mill, an oil field coatings supplier, a plant food company, and a metals recycling operation; but for Houston and his men, it was vegetation as far as the eyes could see.

Today, the location of the crossing that Houston and his men took is filled with oil refineries and chemical plants. The Texas patriots would have a hard time understanding the oil refinery that is now near the spot where they crossed Buffalo Bayou on that patched up old ferry. In his time, the oil business involved whale oil, not petroleum.

What happened to Harrisburg? The original city was located in this area, which has been consumed by the city of Houston. You can still visit and find the historical marker in front of the bank building pictured at the bottom of page 114.

COORDINATES FOR CAMP NEAR HARRISBURG
29.732208911431947 / -95.24164223622634

COORDINATES FOR HARRISBURG
29.7162199978923835 / -95.27793131028368

22 CAPTAIN BACHILLER LOSES HIS CLOTHES

April 18, 1836
Bellaire, Texas

ON APRIL 18, 1836, Houston was camped on the other side of Buffalo Bayou from the burned ruins of Harrisburg. While Houston's men were resting, his scouting party, including Deaf Smith, went out on patrol to look for Santa Anna's army. They rode twelve miles to the west towards the Brazos River.

At this spot (present-day Bellaire Boulevard and 2nd Street), the scouting party accidentally encountered and captured two Mexican couriers and a Texan who had been captured and forced into service as a guide. The Mexican soldiers were carrying a mail pouch to Santa Anna. One of the men was a special courier from Mexico City with deerskin saddlebags stamped "W. B. Travis," meaning that they were probably taken from Travis at the Alamo and used, with a triumphal flare, for Santa Anna's personal mail.

It is never a good idea to be captured, but it can be even worse if you happen to be wearing a fine leather suit of clothes that appeals to your captor. At this spot, Deaf Smith apparently made Capt. Miguel Bachiller, one of the Mexican couriers, disrobe and donate his clothes to the Texan

cause. When they arrived back in camp that evening, the courier was wearing Smith's worn out clothes and shoes, while Smith was dressed in the fine suit of clothes the courier had been wearing.[1] To make the situation more comical, Smith's clothes were baggy on the courier, and the courier's pants were too short for Smith.

The captives and letters were taken back to Houston's camp where they were translated by some of Houston's Tejano soldiers. From the letters, Houston learned that Santa Anna had separated his divisions, giving Houston a temporary advantage to engage the Mexican Army at less than full strength. He also learned that Santa Anna was mistaken about the size of Houston's force; Houston had approximately 1,100 men but Santa Anna thought he only had 650. Also, the Mexican forces did not know the Texans' exact location. The information from the captured letters played a vital role in Houston's decision to fight at San Jacinto. Houston also learned that Gen. Martín Perfecto de Cos was on his way to join Santa Anna with six hundred soldiers.

The site where Deaf Smith and the Texas scouts encountered the Mexican couriers has a historical marker and is in the middle of a residential area, but the location is not well-known because there is no parking in front of the marker. To see the marker, you must park down the road and cross three busy lanes of traffic, so don't visit during rush hour. The marker does a good job of telling the story, but it neglects to mention the part about Captain Bachiller losing his clothes.

COORDINATES FOR CAPT. BACHILLER LOSES HIS CLOTHES
29.70574176834231 / −95.46449523072678

23 ALMOST CHECKMATE

April 18, 1836
Morgan's Point, Texas

INTERIM PRESIDENT of the Republic of Texas David G. Burnet and his cabinet left Harrisburg for New Washington (known today as Morgan's Point) only a few hours before Santa Anna arrived to kill them, a move that would have ended the government of Texas and won the war for Mexico. If this had occurred, Houston's army would have represented nothing; the war would be lost without his army fighting a battle. Santa Anna went for checkmate and was almost successful.

President Burnet, however, had an even closer call when he was leaving New Washington for Galveston. A Mexican cavalry unit of fifty troops commanded by Col. Juan Nepomuceno Almonte had ridden twenty miles from Harrisburg and arrived just as Burnet, his family, and some cabinet members were pulling away from shore in a rowboat to board a steamer. The Texans were about thirty yards away from shore as the Mexicans prepared to shoot, but the Mexican colonel ordered his men to stop because he did not want to kill a woman. Perhaps his good deed was rewarded; Almonte survived the Battle of San Jacinto and was captured alive while swimming in Peggy Lake. Burnet and the government made it to the safety of Galveston.

Santa Anna, and the main body of Mexican soldiers, arrived at New Washington around noon on April 18, 1836, just as Houston arrived at Harrisburg. Angry at missing President Burnet again, Santa Anna had his soldiers loot and burn New Washington.

Santa Anna did find something of interest in New Washington, however—a beautiful young mulatto woman named Emily D. West. He supposedly was charmed when he first saw her loading cargo on the docks. He took her captive and, as the story goes, he was preoccupied with her in his tent on the afternoon of April 21, 1836, when Houston attacked. She is often thought to have been a slave, but records show that she was actually a free indentured servant on the James Morgan

plantation.[1] There are no contemporary accounts of her from the time of the battle; the earliest account is from a British tourist who reported in 1842 of hearing the rumor that she was the reason Santa Anna lost the battle. She is often thought to be the inspiration for the famous song "The Yellow Rose of Texas," although that song was not written until twenty years after the battle. An undocumented rumor does not make good historical research, but it is such a good story that everybody wants it to be true.

I visited Morgan's Point to try and gain some feeling for the location where this exciting escape happened, but alas, industry has taken over. It is now a major shipping container operation. Today, cargo is not unloaded by hand but instead by operators using a computerized crane from the air-conditioned comfort of a control center.

COORDINATES FOR ALMOST CHECKMATE
29.676891443248852 / −94.98158045443277

24 CAMP SAFETY

April 20, 1836
San Jacinto Battleground State Historical Site

AFTER CHEERING the fiery speeches by Houston and Colonel Rusk, the soldiers spent the rest of the day crossing Buffalo Bayou using multiple trips with an improvised log raft and a small leaky boat. There is no historical marker at the crossing's location, although at least one reliable source says there is one.[1] The area is now heavily industrialized and nothing from Houston's time remains.

After crossing the bayou, Houston marched his men all night including crossing the bridge at Vince Bayou in the first two miles. The route was roughly down present-day Lawndale Street.

The goal was to beat Santa Anna to a position that would control Lynch's Ferry. Houston now had a chance for that single decisive battle at a place of his own choosing. He knew that Santa Anna had made the type of fatal error Houston desired—Santa Anna divided his forces in a failed attempt to rush to checkmate, making him vulnerable. His supply chain was extended, and his soldiers were worn out from being in the field so long. Houston knew where to intercept the main Mexican force because Santa Anna still thought that Houston was fleeing to the United States and the ferry was the only way to cross the San Jacinto River—Santa Anna believed Houston had no intention of fighting.

Houston's men stopped around daylight to prepare breakfast. Before they could finish eating, Houston's scouts rode into camp reporting that they had spotted Santa Anna's advance guard nearby. Houston ordered his men back on the march immediately. They reached their selected campsite at 10 a.m., just a few hours before Santa Anna.

The campsite was bordered by water on the rear and both sides, giving the Texans control of the road to Lynch's Ferry. Houston only had to defend his forces from a frontal attack. Perhaps this is why Houston called the location Camp Safety. This site must have reminded him of his camp on the Brazos River where he trained for two weeks, which also provided water protection from three sides. The site dubbed Camp Safety was better, however, because the grove of live oak trees provided

concealment for his troops. Also, unlike the site on the Brazos River, his men were not mired in mud and forced to drink stagnant water.

Shortly after settling into this camp, Houston got lucky. Some of his men on guard saw a small flat boat coming up the bayou. They hid until it got close and then forced the Mexican crew to abandon ship and swim away. Houston's men swam out and took control of what turned out to be a supply boat intended for Santa Anna. The supplies of flour and other food were taken from New Washington before Santa Anna burned the town and were intended to be delivered to the Mexican Army. Houston's men were soon eating Santa Anna's lunch.

The pause in marching gave Houston an opportunity to write a report to President Burnet. Burnet had been demanding that Houston stand and fight, but Houston ignored him and continued the retreat. Now, on the eve of battle, Houston must have taken great pleasure in writing the following report:

TO PRESIDENT BURNET

Camp Safety, San Jacinto, Lynch's Crossing, April 20, 1836.

Mr. President:

Dear Sir — This morning the army reached this point, and was attacked at 1/2 past 11, A. M., by the army of Santa Anna, which continued until 3 o'clock, when he withdrew his forces from the field. Our men were few who engaged the enemy, the balance remaining concealed for the purpose of hiding our number. His force is reported at 800; ours does not exceed 750. I am disposed to think that the enemy intend another attack to-night by a change of position. We had but one man wounded. The enemy's loss is estimated from 18–20. There would be no difficulty in securing the rights of the people and the liberties of Texas, if men would march to their duty, and not fly like recreants from danger. Texas must be defended and liberty maintained.

Sam Houston (Commander-in-Chief)

P.S. Santa Anna was in the field. The officers and Soldiers acted well. Col. Rusk was in the action, and fully met my wishes. H[2]

☞ Getting There ☜

COORDINATES FOR CAMP SAFETY
29.75441476026112 / −95.09038353781011

25 VINCE'S BRIDGE

April 21, 1836
Pasadena, Texas

THE MAIN ROAD from the Brazos River through Harrisburg and on to Lynch's Ferry went through this location. The Vince brothers—William, Allen, Richard, and Robert—built a cedar bridge over Vince Bayou to facilitate travel. That bridge made it easy for Sam Houston to pass by here on his way to his campsite near Lynch's Ferry.

Santa Anna was not so lucky. His army got across the bayou on the bridge, but the stubborn mule pulling his big cannon—The Golden Standard—refused to go on the bridge. The only option was to send Gen. Manuel Fernández Castrillón with the Golden Standard and a company of soldiers to find a place where they could ford the bayou. In essence, the Mexican generals followed a mule's directives. The exact location where the cannon and its guard crossed the river is not known, but it was probably about two miles to the south near where present-day W. Southmore Ave. crosses Vince Bayou and the water level is low enough to wade.

The mule that was afraid of the bridge was not afraid of much else. It pulled the Golden Standard into the front of the battle and was found dead on the field afterwards.

The Road to San Jacinto

On the morning of the battle, April 21, 1836, Deaf Smith and a group of six volunteers destroyed the bridge over Vince Bayou. Some accounts say it was Smith's idea and other accounts give credit to Houston. In either case, Smith would not have done it without Houston's approval. Smith intended to burn the bridge, but most accounts agree that he cut it down with axes because it was too wet to burn well. Removing the bridge cut off the most convenient path of retreat and reinforcement for both armies. Since Houston had no source of reinforcement, he did not need to plan for any. On the other hand, Santa Anna had reinforcements on the way. It may also have been an expression of bravado from an army of civilians about to go into battle against a professional army.

Here is a first-hand account from one of Houston's soldiers:

> Deaf Smith remarked: "That bridge over Vince's ought to be burned down. I will see the General." And two minutes after he

rides up to me saying: "The General thinks it is a good plan." At about two o'clock he returned and I asked him how he succeeded. He said: "I first fired it; but it would not burn; and I then cut away a few timbers and made it fall into the bayou."[1]

I visited at low tide after a dry spell and a large wooden timber was visible just below the water line; could this be the remains of the original cedar bridge at this spot? Could it have survived underwater for 184 years just waiting for me to find it? Maybe nobody else ever looked. A structural engineer informed me that wood can survive underwater for centuries as long as it is not exposed to oxygen. In fact, probably every building in Venice, Italy, is supported on timber piles that are centuries old.

COORDINATES FOR VINCE'S BRIDGE
29.7193659639827735 / -95.22034738788544

COORDINATES FOR WHERE THE GOLDEN STANDARD CROSSED
29.69086974860732 / -95.21783155023233

26 CAPTURE OF SANTA ANNA

April 22, 1836
Pasadena, Texas

WAS ANYTHING ACCOMPLISHED by destroying Vince's Bridge? Yes, but it was not during the battle. The victory was so quick that neither army had any need to consider retreat.

Santa Anna woke from his afternoon siesta and immediately escaped the battle on horseback. His personal secretary Ramon Caro was with him. They almost certainly would have been killed in the chaos of the battle if they had not made a quick escape. They rode straight for Vince's Bridge obviously intending to reach his reinforcements to the west. It might have worked if the bridge was in place. The escape route might still have worked except for one problem: Santa Anna did not know how to swim. He was trapped in the muddy weed-filled area around Vince's Bayou.

The two men had been followed by some Texan soldiers, but they lost Santa Anna in the darkness and thick weeds. They staked out the area all night while Santa Anna hid in the weeds. In the morning, Caro surrendered immediately to the first soldiers he could find, but Santa Anna went on to find an abandoned slave cabin with some old clothes in it. He dressed as a slave, except, of course, for his diamond-studded shirt and red Moroccan slippers—his disguise was about as good as his swimming.

By three o'clock in the afternoon on the day after the battle, a group of Texan soldiers found him in the grass at the location on Buffalo Bayou pictured below. He was about half a mile from Vince's Bridge. The soldiers thought about killing him and probably would have if they had recognized him. The disguise worked until they took him to the prisoner area and the other prisoners immediately responded with joy to see their commander alive.

If Santa Anna had been able to cross Vince Bayou, he might have made it to Gen. Vicente Filisola's forces—four thousand strong in Texas—and organized an attack on Sam Houston. Texas would not be Texas today. Instead, Houston forced Santa Anna to order Filisola to retreat and release

all prisoners. If Santa Anna had been killed, that order never would have been made. It was that close.

Santa Anna was brought to Houston's campsite on Buffalo Bayou. Houston was wounded in the left ankle and lying under an oak tree at this exact spot. While the tree in the photo below is not the same tree Houston sat under, this location is one of the most significant historical sites in Texas because this is where the Texas Revolution ended. Houston first verified that the muddy soldier in front of him was really Santa Anna by having some other captive officers confirm the identification. A translator was brought in and compliant Santa Anna agreed to ceasing all hostilities, withdrawing his troops, and releasing all prisoners. They found his writing desk on the battlefield and his personal secretary penned these agreements on official stationery. On the evening of April 22, 1836, Deaf Smith was asked to deliver copies of the documents to the remaining Mexican forces—the Texas Revolution was over.

Sam Houston had great reverence for this spot. Jeff Hamilton, Houston's former slave who became his lifelong driver, recalled that Houston asked to be driven here in 1863, shortly before his death. Hamilton recalls:

> The General didn't speak a word on the way—he was wrapped up in his own thought. Nor did he say anything to me, as he usually did, when he got to the end of a trip, put painfully alighted from the buggy. We had driven up to the big oak tree where Santa Anna had stood as a prisoner before Genenral Houston.
>
> The General sat on the ground under the tree for a long time, never speaking to me or looking at me. He had a far-off look in his eyes, which I couldn't help but notice were wet.[1]

COORDINATES OF HOUSTON'S CAMP
29.753550114417678 / -95.09088247201859

COORDINATES FOR SANTA ANNA CAPTURE SITE
29.724518446774287 / -95.21286037750241

NOTE: *When visiting this site, be sure to stay to the right on Shaver Street/Federal Road to avoid entering the Washburn Tunnel.*

LIST OF STOPS

LOCATION 1
COORDINATES FOR HOUSTON'S CAMP
29.497140062498819 / -97.45367276160665

LOCATION 2
COORDINATES FOR THE GONZALES MEMORIAL MUSEUM
29.504046008046082 / -97.44341149830777

LOCATION 3
COORDINATES FOR ST. LOUIS STREET
29.507584786675684 / -97.43121918553393

LOCATION 4
COORDINATES FOR PEACH CREEK
29.47403587911124 / −97.316443189981996

LOCATION 5
COORDINATES FOR SAM HOUSTON OAK
29.476189120616755 / −97.3080698146149

LOCATION 6
COORDINATES FOR AMERICAN LEGION HALL IN MOULTON
29.579086734780766 / −97.14343121586357

LOCATION 7
COORDINATES FOR ROCKY CREEK
29.581540793860878 / −96.91829932873303

LOCATION 8
COORDINATES FOR FM 221
29.58603601225505 / −96.91573380947634

LOCATION 9
COORDINATES FOR ORIGINAL AND
CURRENT LOCATION IN FAYETTE CO.
29.801997574590878 / -96.7971395950296

LOCATION 10
COORDINATES FOR STOLEN LOCATION IN COLORADO CO.
29.755464554039584 / -96.73713500553065

LOCATION 11
COORDINATES FOR BURNHAM FERRY ROAD:
29.78581375887209 / -96.72351732048868

LOCATION 12
COORDINATES FOR JERRELL COFFEE ROAD AND ROCKY CREEK
29.7428330307212222 / -96.61723717963098

LOCATION 13
COORDINATES FOR BEASON'S CROSSING PARK
29.705127871258046 / -96.53523224455242

LOCATION 14
COORDINATES FOR THE MEXICAN CAMP
29.705497592945353 / −96.56061242029162

LOCATION 15
COORDINATES FOR THE COLUMBUS OAK
29.70666492874792 / −96.55128281794202

LOCATION 16
COORDINATES FOR CAMP ON MENTZ ROAD
29.740502224076042 / −96.4491786630461

LOCATION 17
COORDINATES FOR THE CAMP IN SAN FELIPE
29.805498737346145 / −96.1215890613063

LOCATION 18
COORDINATES FOR MILL CREEK
29.870234686649559 / −96.155660063381013

LOCATION 19
COORDINATES FOR POTENTIAL BURIAL SITE
29.8866647132863928 / -96.1501478168991

LOCATION 20
COORDINATES FOR POSSIBLE CAMPSITE
30.01568547746856 / -96.1298534257422

LOCATION 21
COORDINATES FOR THE CAMP ON THE BRAZOS
30.009338175594472 / -96.1149198266859

LOCATION 22
COORDINATES FOR HOUSTON MEETING THE TWIN SISTERS
30.006544855249615 / -96.0820913959978

LOCATION 23
COORDINATES FOR DONOHO'S
30.056465344699944 / -96.03813237950045

List of Stops

LOCATION 24
COORDINATES FOR McCARLEY HOMESTEAD
30.0696655676303068 / −95.80706913374306

LOCATION 25
COORDINATES FOR WHICH WAY TREE
30.079515774110728 / −95.76075300723136

LOCATION 26
COORDINATES FOR TELGE PARK
29.95405493251514 / −95.64792082693336

LOCATION 27
COORDINATES FOR CAMPSITE ON APRIL 17
29.806405049598446 / −95.33245481026633

LOCATION 28
COORDINATES FOR CAMP NEAR HARRISBURG
29.732208911431947 / −95.241642223622634

LOCATION 29
COORDINATES FOR HARRISBURG
29.7162199789923835 / -95.27793131028368

LOCATION 30
COORDINATES FOR CAPT. BACHILLER LOSES HIS CLOTHES
29.705741768334231 / -95.46449523072678

LOCATION 31
COORDINATES FOR ALMOST CHECKMATE
29.676891443248852 / -94.98158045443277

LOCATION 32
COORDINATES FOR CAMP SAFETY
29.75441476026112 / -95.09038353781011

LOCATION 33
COORDINATES FOR VINCE'S BRIDGE
29.7193659639982735 / -95.22034738788544

LOCATION 34
COORDINATES FOR WHERE THE GOLDEN STANDARD CROSSED
29.69086974860732 / -95.21783155023233

LOCATION 35
COORDINATES OF HOUSTON'S CAMP
29.753550114417678 / -95.09088247201859

LOCATION 36
COORDINATES FOR SANTA ANNA CAPTURE SITE
29.724518446774287 / -95.21286037750241

EPILOGUE

THERE IS NO NEED to provide a detailed account of the battle as there are many good ones already. Besides, this book is about the lead up to the battle, not the battle itself. Suffice it to say, it was an unequivocal victory for the Texans. The Mexican Army numbering 1,250 lost 630 soldiers killed. The smaller Texan Army totaling 933 men lost eleven soldiers killed. The captured Santa Anna ordered his remaining troops to leave Texas and signed a peace agreement recognizing Texas. Texas was founded as an independent country and stayed that way until it became part of the United States in 1845.

Napoleon would have been proud of Houston for outmaneuvering Santa Anna. This discussion of Napoleon's strategy quoted in Chapter 2 should make more sense now:

> Napoleon placed great emphasis on movement as a part of warfare. This was best demonstrated during his Italian campaign of the 1790s. Taking his troops back and forth across the country, he repeatedly outmaneuvered the Austrians and their Piedmontese allies. It allowed him to fight battles at a time and place that suited him. . . . He pushed the French military toward field guns

which were on average a third lighter than those of their British opponents. This allowed the guns to be moved quickly around the battlefield and used to their best effect. . . . He also focused the power of his guns. Instead of spreading them out to provide support for the infantry, he collected large mobile batteries. Their coordinated firepower could make significant dents in enemy formations. . . . Napoleon aimed to feed his armies from the land rather than transporting large volumes of supplies with them. It had two advantages in supporting his war of movement. Firstly, it meant his armies were unburdened with the weight of supplies and the slowness of wagon trains. Secondly, it made him less dependent on supply lines back to France, making him less vulnerable to enemy maneuvers. . . . Although Napoleon's methods were about outmaneuvering the enemy, his aims were unequivocal. Unlike many of his predecessors, he focused on bringing about the utter destruction of the enemy armies. The goal was not just to defeat or dislodge them. It was to smash them decisively in a single battle, removing their ability to fight and forcing them to negotiation on his terms. . . . The other strategy was the central position. Napoleon used this when he faced more than one enemy or an enemy army that had become divided. By holding a central position, he could split his enemies apart. He would hold one off with a relatively small part of his army, while he defeated the other force.[1]

Sam Houston went on to be elected President of Texas and then governor and senator of the State of Texas. Santa Anna was released back to Mexico where he continued to pursue political power with varied success. Later in his life, Santa Anna played a role in popularizing chewing gum in the United States, though in Texas, Santa Anna will always be best known for his involvement in the Texas Revolution.²

NOTES

SAM HOUSTON TAKES COMMAND
1. Frank X. Tolbert, *The Day of San Jacinto* (Austin and New York: Pemberton Press, 1959), 50.
2. James L. Haley, *Sam Houston* (Norman: University of Oklahoma Press, 2002), 31.
3. "Texas Declaration of Independence, 1836," The Gilder Lehrman Institute of American History website, found online at: *https://www.gilderlehrman.org/history-resources/spotlight-primary-source/texas-declaration-independence-1836*.

HOUSTON'S FIRST BIG DECISION
1. John Holland Jenkins, *Recollections of Early Texas: The Memoirs of John Holland Jenkins*, edited by John Holmes Jenkins III (Austin: University of Texas Press, 1958), 37.
2. Ibid., 39.
3. Andrew Knighton, "8 changes Napoleon made to warfare—one of the most influential generals in history," February 2, 2017, War History Online website, found online at: *https://www.warhistoryonline.com/napoleon/8-changes-napoleon-made-warfare.html*.

RUNAWAY SCRAPE
1. N. D. Labadie, "The San Jacinto Campaign," *Texas Almanac*, 1859, book, University of North Texas Libraries, The Portal to Texas History, found online at: *https://texashistory.unt.edu/ark:/67531/metapth123765/*, page 42.
2. Eugene C. Barker, "The San Jacinto Campaign," *The Quarterly of the State of Texas Historical Association*, Vol. 4, No. 4 (April 1901), 308.

CAMP ON THE LAVACA RIVER

1. Jann Seal, "How to Age a Live Oak Tree," article, Hunker.com website, November 8, 2021, found online at: *https://www.hunker.com/12542585/how-to-age-a-live-oak-tree*.
2. John Holland Jenkins, *Recollections of Early Texas: The Memoirs of John Holland Jenkins*, edited by John Holmes Jenkins III (Austin: University of Texas Press, 1958), 39.
3. James K. Baker, "The Lavaca River Trench and Lost Cannon," *Journal of South Texas*, Vol. 22, No. 2 (2009), 145–54.
4. John M. Swisher, "The Swisher Memoirs," text, date unknown, University of North Texas Libraries, The Portal to Texas History, found online at: *https://texashistory.unt.edu/ark:/67531/metapth32349/*, see pages 31–32.
5. C. W. Pressler and H. M. Bramlette, Lavaca Co., map, 1914, Austin, Texas, University of North Texas Libraries, The Portal to Texas History, found online at: *https://texashistory.unt.edu/ark:/67531/metapth493034/*.

PRIVATE RHODES HAS A BAD DAY

1. Eugene C. Barker, "The San Jacinto Campaign," *The Quarterly of the State of Texas Historical Association*, Vol. 4, No. 4 (April 1901), 296.
2. Stephen L. Moore, *Eighteen Minutes: The Battle of San Jacinto and the Texas Independence Campaign* (Dallas: Republic of Texas Press, 2004), 453.
3. Barker, "The San Jacinto Campaign," 318.

ROAD TO NAVIDAD

1. Stephen L. Moore, *Eighteen Minutes: The Battle of San Jacinto and the Texas Independence Campaign* (Dallas: Republic of Texas Press, 2004), 71.

BURNHAM'S FERRY

1. J. H. Kuykendall, "Recollections of the Campaign," Eugene C. Barker, ed., *The Quarterly of the Texas State Historical Association*, Texas State Historical Association, Vol. 4, No. 4 (April 1901), 297.
2. Stephen L. Moore, *Eighteen Minutes: The Battle of San Jacinto and the Texas Independence Campaign* (Dallas: Republic of Texas Press, 2004), 41.
3. Mosley Baker, "Mosley Baker's Letter to Houston," *The Quarterly of the Texas Historical Association*, Vol. 4, No. 4 (April 1901), 275.
4. "Crier, John," *Handbook of Texas Online*, website, Texas State Historical Association, found online at: *https://www.tshaonline.org/handbook/entries/crier-john*.

TRAVELING IN THE RAIN

1   J. H. Kuykendall, "Recollections of the Campaign," Eugene C. Barker, ed., *The Quarterly of the Texas State Historical Association*, Texas State Historical Association, Vol. 4, No. 4 (April 1901), 244.

CAMPING BY A SPRING

1   N. D. Labadie, "The San Jacinto Campaign," *Texas Almanac*, 1859, book, University of North Texas Libraries, The Portal to Texas History, found online at: *https://texashistory.unt.edu/ark:/67531/metapth123765/*, p. 44.

2   Stephen L. Moore, *Eighteen Minutes: The Battle of San Jacinto and the Texas Independence Campaign* (Dallas: Republic of Texas Press, 2004), 128; J. H. Kuykendall, "Recollections of the Campaign," Eugene C. Barker, ed., *The Quarterly of the Texas State Historical Association*, Texas State Historical Association, Vol. 4, No. 4 (April 1901), 300.

3   Labadie, p. 44.

4   Ibid.

5   Ibid.

6   Kuykendall, 300.

7   Labadie, p. 44.

8   Ibid.

SAN FELIPE

1   J. H. Kuykendall, "Recollections of the Campaign," Eugene C. Barker, ed., *The Quarterly of the Texas State Historical Association*, Texas State Historical Association, Vol. 4, No. 4 (April 1901), 300.

2   N. D. Labadie, "The San Jacinto Campaign," *Texas Almanac*, 1859, book, University of North Texas Libraries, The Portal to Texas History, found online at: *https://texashistory.unt.edu/ark:/67531/metapth123765/*, p. 44.

3   Henry Stuart Foote, *Texas and the Texans: Or, Advance of the Anglo-Americans to the South-west; Including a History of Leading Events in Mexico, from the Conquest by Fernando Cortes to the Termination of the Texas Revolution* (Philadelphia: Thomas, Cowperthwait & Company, 1841), 283.

MUDDY MILL CREEK

1   J. H. Kuykendall, "Recollections of the Campaign," Eugene C. Barker, ed., *The Quarterly of the Texas State Historical Association*, Texas State Historical Association, Vol. 4, No. 4 (April 1901), 301.

2   Kuykendall, 298.

VICTORY OR DEATH AT RACCOON BEND

1. William Physick Zuber, *My Eighty Years in Texas*, edited by Janis Boyle Mayfield (Austin, University of Texas Press, 1971), 67; J. H. Kuykendall, "Recollections of the Campaign," Eugene C. Barker, ed., *The Quarterly of the Texas State Historical Association*, Texas State Historical Association, Vol. 4, No. 4 (April 1901), 301.
2. Zuber, 67.
3. Ibid.
4. Google Maps satellite view.
5. Zuber, 66; Kuykendall, 301.

BASIC TRAINING ON THE BRAZOS

1. Sam Houston, *The Writings of Sam Houston*, Amelia W. Williams and Eugene C. Baker, eds., Volume II (Austin: The University of Texas Press, 1939), 23–24.
2. Stephen L. Moore, *Eighteen Minutes: The Battle of San Jacinto and the Texas Independence Campaign* (Dallas: Republic of Texas Press, 2004), 163.

HOUSTON MEETS THE TWIN SISTERS

1. Stephen L. Moore, *Eighteen Minutes: The Battle of San Jacinto and the Texas Independence Campaign* (Dallas: Republic of Texas Press, 2004), 174.
2. N. D. Labadie, "The San Jacinto Campaign," *Texas Almanac*, 1859, book, University of North Texas Libraries, The Portal to Texas History, found online at: *https://texashistory.unt.edu/ark:/67531/metapth123765/*, p. 46.

McCARLEY'S HOME

1. "Samuel McCarley Homesite," Description on Texas Historical Marker 10726, Atlas Number 520101726, Texas State Historical Commission, Atlas website, found online at: *https://atlas.thc.state.tx.us/*.

FORK IN THE ROAD

1. Stephen L. Moore, *Eighteen Minutes: The Battle of San Jacinto and the Texas Independence Campaign* (Dallas: Republic of Texas Press, 2004), 176.
2. N. D. Labadie, "The San Jacinto Campaign," *Texas Almanac*, 1859, book, University of North Texas Libraries, The Portal to Texas History, found online at: *https://texashistory.unt.edu/ark:/67531/metapth123765/*, p. 47–48.
3. Noah Smithwick, *The Evolution of a State or Recollections of Old Texas Days* (Austin: Gammel Book Company, 1900), 208–209.

TELGE PARK, THE CAPITOL OF TEXAS (FOR A DAY)

1. S. F. Sparks, "Recollections of S. F. Sparks," *The Quarterly of the Texas State Historical Association*, Texas State Historical Association, Vol. 12 (July 1908–April, 1909), 68–69, University of North Texas Libraries, The Portal to Texas History, found online at: *https://texashistory.unt.edu/ark:/67531/metapth101048/*.

WHERE DID SAM HOUSTON'S ARMY CAMP ON APRIL 17, 1836?

1. Mosley Baker, "Extracts from Mosley Baker's Letter to Houston," *Texas Almanac*, 1859, book, University of North Texas Libraries, The Portal to Texas History, found online at: *https://texashistory.unt.edu/ark:/67531/metapth123765/*, p. 283.
2. J. H. Kuykendall, "Recollections of the Campaign," Eugene C. Barker, ed., *The Quarterly of the Texas State Historical Association*, Texas State Historical Association, Vol. 4, No. 4 (April 1901), 303.
3. Ibid.
4. N. D. Labadie, "The San Jacinto Campaign," *Texas Almanac*, 1859, book, University of North Texas Libraries, The Portal to Texas History, found online at: *https://texashistory.unt.edu/ark:/67531/metapth123765/*, p. 43.
5. Google Maps.
6. Google Maps.

CAMP NEAR HARRISBURG

1. S. F. Sparks, "Recollections of S. F. Sparks," *The Quarterly of the Texas State Historical Association*, Texas State Historical Association, Vol. 12 (July 1908–April 1909), p. 70, University of North Texas Libraries, The Portal to Texas History, found online at: *https://texashistory.unt.edu/ark:/67531/metapth101048/*.
2. Sam Houston, *The Writings of Sam Houston*, Amelia W. Williams and Eugene C. Baker, eds., Volume II (Austin: The University of Texas Press, 1939), 24.
3. N. D. Labadie, "The San Jacinto Campaign," *Texas Almanac*, 1859, book, University of North Texas Libraries, The Portal to Texas History, found online at: *https://texashistory.unt.edu/ark:/67531/metapth123765/*, p. 49.

CAPTAIN BACHILLER LOSES HIS CLOTHES

1. Stephen L. Moore, *Eighteen Minutes: The Battle of San Jacinto and the Texas Independence Campaign* (Dallas: Republic of Texas Press, 2004), 239.

ALMOST CHECKMATE

1. Stephen L. Moore, *Eighteen Minutes: The Battle of San Jacinto and the Texas Independence Campaign* (Dallas: Republic of Texas Press, 2004), 416.

CAMP SAFETY

1. Stephen L. Moore, *Eighteen Minutes: The Battle of San Jacinto and the Texas Independence Campaign* (Dallas: Republic of Texas Press, 2004), 251.
2. Sam Houston, *The Writings of Sam Houston*, Amelia W. Williams and Eugene C. Baker, eds., Volume II (Austin: The University of Texas Press, 1939), 24.

VINCE'S BRIDGE

1. N. D. Labadie, "Labadie's Account of the Campaign," Eugene C. Barker, ed., *The Quarterly of the Texas State Historical Association*, Texas State Historical Association, Vol. 4, No. 4 (April 1901), 315.

CAPTURE OF SANTA ANNA

1. Jeff Hamilton, as told to Lenoir Hunt, *My Master: The Inside Story of Sam Houston and his Times* (Austin: State House Press, 1992), 93.

EPILOGUE

1. Andrew Knighton, "8 changes Napoleon made to warfare—one of the most influential generals in history," February 2, 2017, War History Online website, found online at: *https://www.warhistoryonline.com/napoleon/8-changes-napoleon-made-warfare.html*.
2. Claudia Geib, "How an Exiled Mexican President Accidentally Invented Chewing Gum," Eater.com website, March 23, 2022, found online at: *https://www.eater.com/22993171/general-antonio-lopez-de-santa-anna-accidentally-created-chewing-gum-gastropod*.

BIBLIOGRAPHY

PRIMARY SOURCES

Austin County. Map. 1838. University of North Texas Libraries. The Portal to Texas History. Found online at: *https://texashistory.unt.edu/ark:/67531/metapth88326/*.

Austin County. Map. 1860. University of North Texas Libraries. The Portal to Texas History. Found online at: *https://texashistory.unt.edu/ark:/67531/metapth88327/*.

Baker, Mosley. "Extracts from Mosley Baker's Letter to Houston." *Texas Almanac*. 1859. Book. University of North Texas Libraries. The Portal to Texas History. Found online at: *https://texashistory.unt.edu/ark:/67531/metapth123765/*.

Baker, Mosley. "Mosley Baker's Letter to Houston." *The Quarterly of the Texas Historical Association*. Vol. 4, No. 4 (April 1901).

"Crier, John." *Handbook of Texas Online*. Website. Texas State Historical Association. Found online at: *https://www.tshaonline.org/handbook/entries/crier-john*.

Hamilton, Jeff. As told to Lenoir Hunt. *My Master: The Inside Story of Sam Houston and his Times*. Austin: State House Press, 1992.

Hunter, Robert Hancock. *The Narrative of Robert Hancock Hunter*. Austin: The Encino Press, 1966.

Jenkins, John Holland. *Recollections of Early Texas: The Memoirs of John Holland Jenkins*. Edited by John Holmes Jenkins III. Austin: University of Texas Press, 1958.

Kuykendall, J. H. "Recollections of the Campaign," Eugene C. Barker, ed. *The Quarterly of the Texas State Historical Association.* Texas State Historical Association. Vol. 4, No. 4 (April 1901).

Labadie, N. D. "Labadie's Account of the Campaign." Eugene C. Barker, ed. *The Quarterly of the Texas State Historical Association.* Texas State Historical Association. Vol. 4, No. 4 (April 1901).

Labadie, N. D. "The San Jacinto Campaign." *Texas Almanac.* Book. 1859. University of North Texas Libraries. The Portal to Texas History. Found online at: *https://texashistory.unt.edu/ark:/67531/metapth123765/*.

Martin, Joseph. Lavaca County. Map. January 30, 1866. University of North Texas Libraries. The Portal to Texas History. Found online at: *https://texashistory.unt.edu/ark:/67531/metapth88768/m1/1/*.

McDonald, H. F., and J. Bascom Giles. Colorado County. Map. 1920. Austin, Texas. University of North Texas Libraries. The Portal to Texas History. Found online at: *https://texashistory.unt.edu/ark:/67531/metapth493653/*.

Olmsted, Frederick Law. *A Journey Through Texas: or a Saddle-Trip on the Southwestern Frontier.* Dix, Edwards & Co., 1857; rpt. Coppell, TX: 2018.

Pressler, Charles W. Lavaca County. Map. October 1853. University of North Texas Libraries. The Portal to Texas History. Found online at: *https://texashistory.unt.edu/ark:/67531/metapth88766/*.

Pressler, C. W., and H. M. Bramlette. Lavaca County. Map. 1914. Austin, Texas. University of North Texas Libraries. The Portal to Texas History. Found online at: *https://texashistory.unt.edu/ark:/67531/metapth493034/*.

Pressler, Herman and J. W. Morris. Waller County. Map. 1900. University of North Texas Libraries. The Portal to Texas History. Found online at: *https://texashistory.unt.edu/ark:/67531/metapth492985/*.

Seguin, Juan. *A Revolution Remembered.* Jesus F. de la Teja, ed. Austin: Texas State Historical Association, 2002.

Smithwick, Noah. *The Evolution of a State or Recollections of Old Texas Days.* Austin: Gammel Book Company, 1900.

Sparks, S. F. "Recollections of S. F. Sparks." *The Quarterly of the Texas State Historical Association*. Texas State Historical Association. Vol. 12 (July 1908–April, 1909), 68–69. University of North Texas Libraries. The Portal to Texas History. Found online at: *https://texashistory.unt.edu/ark:/67531/metapth101048/*.

Swisher, John M. "The Swisher Memoirs." Text. Date unknown. University of North Texas Libraries. The Portal to Texas History. Found online at: *https://texashistory.unt.edu/ark:/67531/metapth32349/*.

"Texas Declaration of Independence, 1836." The Gilder Lehrman Institute of American History. Website. Found online at: *https://www.gilderlehrman.org/history-resources/spotlight-primary-source/texas-declaration-independence-1836*.

Upshur, Horace L. Colorado County. Map. 1841. University of North Texas Libraries. The Portal to Texas History. Found online at: *https://texashistory.unt.edu/ark:/67531/metapth88281/*.

Upshur, Horace L. Fayette County. Map. 1843. University of North Texas Libraries. The Portal to Texas History. Found online at: *https://texashistory.unt.edu/ark:/67531/metapth88545/*.

Zuber, William Physick. *My Eighty Years in Texas*. Edited by Janis Boyle Mayfield. Austin, University of Texas Press, 1971.

SECONDARY SOURCES

Anonymous. *The Life of Sam Houston, the Hunter, Patriot, and Statesman of Texas*. Philadelphia: John Potter and Company, 1867.

Aulbach, Louis F. *Buffalo Bayou: An Echo of Houston's Wilderness Beginnings*. Houston: Louis F. Aulbach, 2012.

Baker, James K. "The Lavaca River Trench and Lost Cannon." *Journal of South Texas*. Vol. 22, No. 2 (2009), 145–54.

Barker, Eugene C. "The San Jacinto Campaign." *The Quarterly of the State of Texas Historical Association*. Vol. 4, No. 4 (April 1901), 237–345.

Campbell, Randolph B. *Gone to Texas: A History of the Lone Star State*. New York: Oxford University Press, 2012.

Fehrenbach, T. R. *Lone Star: A History of Texas and the Texans.* New York: American Legacy Press, 1983.

Foote, Henry Stuart. *Texas and the Texans: Or, Advance of the Anglo-Americans to the Southwest; Including a History of Leading Events in Mexico, from the Conquest by Fernando Cortes to the Termination of the Texas Revolution.* Philadelphia: Thomas, Cowperthwait & Company, 1841.

Geib, Claudia. "How an Exiled Mexican President Accidentally Invented Chewing Gum." Eater.com website. March 23, 2022. Found online at: *https://www.eater .com/22993171/general-antonio-lopez-de-santa-anna-accidentally-created-chewing -gum-gastropod.*

Google Maps. Website. Alphabet Corporation. Found online at: *https://www.google .com/maps.*

Haley, James L. *Sam Houston.* Norman: University of Oklahoma Press, 2002.

Hardin, Stephen L. *Texian Iliad: A Military History of the Texas Revolution.* Austin: University of Texas Press, 2004.

Kilmeade, Brian. *Sam Houston and the Alamo Avengers.* New York: Sentinel, 2019.

Knighton, Andrew. "8 changes Napoleon made to warfare—one of the most influential generals in history." Article. War History Online website. February 2, 2017. Found online at: *https://www.warhistoryonline.com/napoleon/8-changes -napoleon-made-warfare.html.*

McDonald, Archie P. *The Trail to San Jacinto.* Boston: American Press, 1982.

Moore, Stephen L. *Eighteen Minutes: The Battle of San Jacinto and the Texas Independence Campaign.* Dallas: Republic of Texas Press, 2004.

Muir, Andrew Forest, ed. *Texas in 1837.* Austin: University of Texas Press, 1986.

Newell, Chester. *History of the Revolution in Texas: Particularly of the War of 1835 and '36.* New York: Wiley & Putnam, 1838.

Portal to Texas History. Website. University of North Texas Libraries. Found online at: *https://texashistory.unt.edu/.*

Seal, Jann. "How to Age a Live Oak Tree." Article. Hunker.com website. November 8, 2021. Found online at: *https://www.hunker.com/12542585/how-to-age-a-live-oak-tree*.

Texas Historic Sites Atlas. Website. Texas Historical Commission. Found online at: *https://atlas.thc.state.tx.us/Map*.

Tolbert, Frank X. *The Day of San Jacinto*. Austin and New York: Pemberton Press, 1959.

United States Geological Survey (USGS). Website. United States Department of the Interior. Found online at: *https://apps.nationalmap.gov/downloader/#/*.

Williams, Amelia W. and Eugene C. Baker, eds. *The Writings of Sam Houston*. Volume II. Austin: The University of Texas Press, 1939.

Williams, Amelia. *Following General Sam Houston from 1793 to 1863*. Austin: The Steck Company, 1935.

Wood, Michael. *In the Footsteps of Alexander the Great*. Berkeley: University of California Press, 2001.

Woodrick, Jim. "Texas History Snippets." Blog. Found online at: *http://texashistorysnippets.blogspot.com/*.

INDEX

A
Alamo, viii, 3, 7, 8, 29, 76, 77, 113, 116,
Almonte, Col. Juan Neupomuceno, 119
American Declaration of Independence, 2
Atascocito, 66

B
Bachiller, Capt. Miguel, 116, 118
Baker, Mosley, 39
Batterson, Isaac, 111, 115
Beason, Benjamin, 45
Beason's Crossing, 45
Bellaire, Texas, 116
Big Rocky Creek, 24–25, 27
Bird, Capt. John, 15
Bonaparte, Napoleon, 10–11, 41, 143–44
Bowie, James, 29
Brazos River, 62, 65, 71, 78, 83, 86, 116, 123–24, 126
Buffalo Bayou, 106, 107, 111, 113, 115–16, 131–32
Bullinger Creek, 60
Burnet, David, 80, 99–100, 103, 105–106, 119–20, 124
Burnett's Plantation, 99–100, 103, 105–106

Burnham, Jesse, 36
Burnham's Ferry, 36
Burnham Ferry Road, 39

C
Camp Safety, 123–24
Caro, Ramon, 130
Castrillon, Gen. Manuel Fernandez, 126
Cherokee Indians, 1, 49
Cincinnati, Ohio, 81–82, 85, 90
Cincinnatus, 82, 85
Colorado County, 33–34, 36–37
Colorado River, 37, 39, 41–42, 46, 66
Columbus, Texas, 41–42, 45, 51
Cos, Gen. Martin Perfecto de, 118
Crier Creek, 39
Crier, John, 37, 39, 40–41

D
Daniels, Williamson, 21, 23, 27
Deaf Smith, 7, 116, 118, 128, 132
Dickenson, Susannah, 7
Donoho, Charles, 86–88
Donoho's Plantation, 86–88

E
Esar Road, 64

F

Fannin, James, 7, 41, 45, 48, 52, 60
Fayette County, 33–34, 37
Filisola, General Vicente, 131
Foote, Henry Stuart, 63
Fort Bend, Texas, 62, 86

G

Galena Park, Texas, 106, 108, 111–12
Galveston, Texas, 82, 119
Garner, John, 79, 80
Golden Standard, 84, 126,
Goliad, viii, 8, 46, 48, 49, 62, 74, 77
Gonzales, Texas, vii, 1–3, 5, 7–9, 13–14, 16, 18, 23–24, 27, 39–41
Groce, Jared, 71,78, 83, 86
Groce's Landing, 65, 86
Guadalupe River, 5, 9

H

Harrisburg, Texas, 82, 93–96, 99, 103, 105–106, 111–16, 119–20, 126
Hempstead, Texas, 82, 85, 88
Hockley, Col. George Washington, 80, 90
Houston Oak, 15, 18
Houston, City of, 106
Houston, Sam, vii–ix, 1–5, 7, 10, 13, 45, 51–52, 77, 81, 85–86, 88, 90, 93, 97, 99, 105, 107, 110, 113,
125–26, 131, 133, 144
Hunting Bayou, 107, 108, 110

J

Jackson, Andrew, 2
Jerrell Coffee Road, 43
John Fairey Garden, 87

K

Kashmere Gardens, 108, 110
Kuykendall, J. H., 25, 53, 60, 66, 71, 74

L

Labadie, Dr. N. D., 53–55, 95–96, 113
Lavaca County, 23, 27
Lavaca River, 18, 23
Lower Rocky Creek, 24
Lynch's Ferry, 111, 122–24, 126

M

Mann, Pamelia, 97
Martin, Wyly, 62
McCarley, Samuel, 90, 91
McClure, Barthalamew, 15
Mentz Road, 58
Mentz, Texas, 52
Mill Creek, 65, 69
Morgan, James, 120
Morgan's Point, Texas, 119, 121
Moulton, Texas, 18, 21

N

Nacogdoches, 2, 93
Nashville Dramatic Club, 1
Navidad River, 23, 27, 29
New Kentucky Park, Texas, 96
New Washington, Texas 119, 120, 124

O

Oakland, Texas, 31

P

Peach Creek, 15

R

Raccoon Bend, Texas, 71, 74, 77, 82
Rhodes, Pvt. John, 23–25
Roberts, Abraham, 94–95
Rocky Creek, 43
Runaway Scrape, 14–15, 25, 45
Rusk, Secretary of War Tom, 80, 101, 113, 122, 125

S

Sabine River, 76
San Felipe, Texas, 53, 54, 60, 62, 63, 64, 69
San Jacinto River, 123
Santa Anna, vii, 8, 10, 13, 16, 42, 46, 52, 74, 84, 86, 90, 93–95, 99, 105, 111, 116–26, 128, 130–33, 143–45
Scales, Pvt. Abraham, 79
Seguin, Juan, 112
Sesma, Gen. Joaquin Ramirez y, 46, 49
Shaw's Bend Rd., 43
Sherman, Capt. Sidney, 46, 82
Smith, Maj. Ben F., 54, 95
Smith, Maj. Leander, 82
Smithwick, Noah, 97
Sparks, S. F., 100, 101
Splane, Capt. Peyton R., 29
Spring Creek, 53, 60
St. Louis Street, 9
Stephen F. Austin, 45

T

Telge Park, 103
Tennessee, 2
Texas Declaration of Independence, 2
Texas Historical Commission, 33–34
Texas Piney Woods, 107–108

Thompson, William, 27, 29
Travis, William B., 7, 76, 116
Twin Sisters, 81, 82, 83–85, 90, 97, 106, 112

U

United States, 91, 93, 122, 143, 145
Urrea, Gen. Jose de, 48

V

Vince Bayou, 122, 126, 128, 131
Vince's Bridge, 131

W

War of 1812, 2, 14, 19
Washington, George, 82
West, Emily D., 120
Williams, S. M., 60
Woodland Heights, 105–106, 110
Wright, Pvt. Felix G., 65–67, 69, 71, 72

Y

"Yellow Rose of Texas," 121
Yellowstone, 78, 83

Z

Zuber, William, 71–72, 74

www.ingramcontent.com/pod-product-compliance
Lightning Source LLC
Chambersburg PA
CBHW071242070526
44583CB00017B/2289